Letters
from a Hermit

With Letters from Matthew Kelty, O.C.S.O.

by William O. Paulsell

TEMPLEGATE PUBLISHERS
Springfield, Illinois 62705

Some selections from these writings have appeared
before in the following publications:
Cistercian Studies
National Catholic Reporter
Katallagete
Monastic Exchange
Crucible

Published by
TEMPLEGATE PUBLISHERS
302 East Adams Street, P.O. Box 963
Springfield, Illinois 62705

ISBN 87243-086-3

Table of Contents

Preface

One morning in the fall of 1973 a student entered my office carrying a large cardboard box. "Father Matthew wants you to have this," she said, as she placed it on my desk.

The student was Judy Broyal from Oxford, North Carolina. Just a few miles from her home is the Monastery of the Holy Mother of God, an experimental Trappist community. At that time the monastery was led by Father Matthew Kelty from the Abbey of Gethsemani in Kentucky. He was leaving for Papua New Guinea where he would take up the life of a hermit.

Judy's brother, Jerry, had been a student in several of my courses at Atlantic Christian College and was a frequent visitor at the monastery. Father Matthew had come to our campus to speak on one occasion and some of the students had developed deep friendships with him. So did I. I made many retreats at the little Oxford monastery while Matthew was there and found his spiritual direction stimulating and enriching.

The cardboard box was a treasure-trove. It contained Matthew's personal papers: sermons, retreat talks, pages from his journal, and a few letters as well as pictures and maps of New Guinea. As I turned slowly through the pages in that box I gradually realized that a man's whole life was spread out on my desk.

This book is not a biography, but an effort to describe one individual's spiritual pilgrimage. The focus is not really on the man, but upon those forces which led him into a deep quest for God in silence, solitude, and seclusion. These are forces which enter the life of every person. The only thing unusual about Matthew is the way in which he responded to them.

The best part of the book, of course, is the last chapter which consists of letters he has written from his New Guinea hermitage. In these we catch an intimate glimpse of the thoughts, feelings, and experiences of one who has left all to find God.

Everything in the book can be documented, but I have chosen to spare the reader the burden of footnotes to material that is not publicly available anyway. Quotations from his papers have been used generously in an effort to capture the spirit of the man more accurately.

When I asked Matthew for permission to do this book he replied, "If you do it or not, it makes no difference." He seeks no publicity for his life. In fact, he would prefer total obscurity. But his experience can help illumine our own confrontations with God, and it is in this way I hope this book will be helpful.

I.
Missionary and Monk

Matthew Kelty is a witty, restless, smiling Irishman from Boston who loves to be around people. He is an excellent public speaker, an engaging conversationalist, and attracts friends in large numbers by his lively manner and warm personality. No one is a stranger to him. He is frequently outspoken, sometimes scornful of convention, and occasionally controversial.

Matthew Kelty lives as a hermit on the northern coast of Papua New Guinea.

What would cause a man like that to take up with solitude? Everyone who knew him realized that such a life was contrary to his whole nature. The story of his move from a Boston suburb to the cabin of a recluse is one of a long tortuous inner struggle. Although looking back over his career one sees a definite trend, a steadily narrowing of the focus of his life, there were many obstacles on the journey to solitude. It did not, at the time it began, seem to be a natural journey.

Matthew is a Sagittarius, born on November 25, 1915, the third of four children. Later in life he expressed a sense of guilt over not having been closer to his family. A career in religion often makes regular family contact difficult, and Matthew confessed that his family had made "many and real" sacrifices for him. He had put his service to God before the interests of his family and hoped that his kin had been spiritually blessed because of it.

Except for a year in Maine, Matthew lived his childhood in Milton, Massachusetts, a suburb of about sixteen thousand people, located just south of Boston. At that time it was largely Protestant with a few Catholic families beginning to move into the area. He described it as "old time Protestant, prim, proper, and really a very lovely town, mostly homes and huge shade trees everywhere." During his twelve years in the public schools there he was taught by "very upright, noble, dedicated women who made a life work of teaching. Not exactly a light-hearted merry group." The few Catholic families in Milton tried hard to fit into the style of the area.

Still, the influence of the Roman Catholic Church was strong, if not always steady, in Matthew's life. In 1934 he entered the Society of the Divine Word (SVD), a missionary order. Matthew described himself as an introvert in his teenage years, but his seminary training developed another side of his personality. "I had to adapt and to adjust in order to survive and so cultivated out-going qualities with zest." He was active in drama, publications, music, debate, clubs, and endless arguments and discussions. He also enjoyed manual work on a farm which taught him skills he would find useful later. What kind of student was he?

"In my studies I was about average and had to work hard, not really knowing how to study."

Matthew progressed normally through the various steps of his training. His first vows were taken in 1941 and he was ordained as a priest in 1946.

His first foreign mission assignment was to New

Guinea. Matthew arrived in that primitive land in January, 1948, never suspecting that he would return there twenty-five years later to live as a hermit. He entered into his work with enthusiasm, happy to be there. "I was pleased. It was far away, had a romantic appeal, involved a primitive people I imagined I could relate to more easily than to some cultured nation."

The assignment was to assist an older missionary in a bush station. Matthew and the pastor took turns going off on two to three week trips into the bush. They would erect primitive chapels, give instruction, dispense medicine, and administer the sacraments. "At first we had few books and papers, no radio, no music, no ice-box, little European food. We managed well enough, but it was arduous; we expected it to be that way."

Much of the time Matthew was alone, and that proved to be a problem. Solitude was far different from the rich community life of seminary days, and Matthew found himself completely unprepared for the loneliness of the mission field. "Sometimes when evening was coming on I could feel a great dark cloud settling on my soul like an oppressive weight."

Matthew began to have doubts that he was in the right place. His SVD training had conditioned him to accept his situation, whatever it might be. It would have been unthinkable to ask for a change. But there was nothing wrong with praying about it. One night he went into the mission chapel and prayed, "You see how things are. You love me. If this is not going to work, get me out of here."

The SVD was aware that Matthew possessed distinct gifts in the use of the written word. In 1951 he was called back to the States to edit *The Christian Family*, the Society mission journal. He had mixed feelings about the change. "I took off from the grass covered air-strip in Madang and waved to a handful of my fellow missionaries. My own heart was very sick, for I had been called back to the USA to do nothing more wonderful than work on a magazine, leaving them there in that place to carry on as best they could. I was indeed no great loss, but every little bit helps in that kind of situation."

Work in an editorial office in Techny, Illinois was a welcomed relief from the loneliness of the mission field, but Matthew remained unsatisfied. Providentially, the SVD dropped the magazine in 1960, and it was clear that Matthew's life was going to change. He felt himself drawn to contemplative monasticism. The intense community life would not have the problems of loneliness he had found in New Guinea, yet would offer a better context for a deeper spiritual life than an editorial office.

In his search for a suitable monastic community Matthew made a retreat at one of the most famous monasteries in the world. The Abbey of Gethsemani, nestled in the rolling hills of Nelson County, Kentucky, was founded by a group of French monks in 1848. It is a house of the Order of Cistercians of the Strict Observance, popularly called the Trappist Order, and has long been known for the austerity and penitential character of its life. In recent years some of its practices have been moderated, but the monastery still maintains its reputation for a rather severe life style.

The best known resident of Gethsemani in the twentieth century was Thomas Merton. Father Louis, as he was known in the monastery, lived there from 1941 until his death in 1968. Through his fifty-five books and hundreds of articles he became one of American Catholicism's most popular spiritual writers. His autobiography, *The Seven Storey Mountain*, was a best seller, popularizing Trappist life and attracting large numbers of men to Gethsemani.

During his retreat Matthew was interviewed and admitted to the community. Returning to Techny he sought and received permission to become a monk. A short time later he passed through the gatehouse at Gethsemani, fully expecting to live the rest of his life there. "They accepted me quietly, without fuss, neither much impressed nor unduly remote. It was all a matter of fact and unexciting. Yet I knew a door had slammed shut behind me." The drab exterior walls of the monastery seemed a strong contrast to the lively spirited personality of Matthew Kelty.

What led Matthew into an austere contemplative institution? He gave one answer in a retreat talk at a sister monastery almost ten years later. "To me, the monastic life has but one purpose and that is to discover reality. In order to discover reality one must remove from one's vision what is false and fraudulent, the artificial and the constructed. Most everyone wants to do this, so monks are not freaks for wishing to discover the truth, but it is far more difficult than it would seem and that is why not everyone is willing to go to the trouble of being a monk, or even once in that area, willing to stay with it. It is hard. Let us face it, it is hard."

Matthew believed that what the world had to offer was deceptive. The monastic life made it possible for him to strip away the maximum number of distractions from his life and get closer to reality, which is God.

In an article appearing in the last issue of *Cistercian Studies* for 1974 he wrote again about the purpose of the monastic life, now seen from his hermitage in New Guinea. "The monk, by virtue of his calling, enters deeply into the human heart and therefore into the human scene.

He at once experiences his own poverty and sinfulness with intensity, and responds to the grace of God in Christ to receive from Him mercy and love. In this dialogue he functions not as himself, as individual person, but as man, and by this identity with man in grace and nature, he sees his relationship to God as something that bears deep relationships also to the entire human family. Thus the monk in no way sees himself as someone else set aside to 'pray for others', or to 'do penance for others', let alone as one called to some higher form of mystical life — he sees himself rather as a sinful man who stands before God and receives mercy."

It was at Gethsemani that Matthew was given his name. He had been born Charles Kelty, and members of the SVD still call him Charlie. But a monk receives a new name, and his was Matthew. Later, when applying for passport and visa the confusion of names would be a minor problem.

When Matthew entered there were "a dozen or so novices." The group included two priests, an artist, an engineer, several young men just out of high school, and men who had worked for Ford and U.S. Steel. Not all would persevere.

Matthew's novice master, the one who trained him in the monastic life, was Thomas Merton. Matthew described him as "at ease, off-handish, sharp, somewhat British." One feature of the novice training was a private interview with the novice master every two weeks. Matthew loved those sessions with Merton. "He was very patient. I do not see how he put up with me, so conceited, so cock-sure, so thin a veneer of education and pomposity."

Later, the new monk would write to a friend, "the novitiate was very difficult for me." It was quite a change from an active apostolate in the world, and Gethsemani never completely succeeded in restraining his active spirit. But as he would tell some of his Gethsemani brothers later, "I came here for deeper religious life, deeper community life, liturgy, and prayer. I found all I came for and have been very happy here."

Matthew lived at Gethsemani during a time of transition that for many monks was traumatic. The year before he entered Pope John XXIII had issued a call for the Second Vatican Council. No one could foresee the sweeping changes that would come over Roman Catholicism in the wake of that Council.

At Gethsemani the changes were drastic. The liturgy shifted from Latin to English and became less complex. New music had to be written. The distinction between choir monks who were priests and lay brothers was virtually abolished by a Decree of Unification. The buildings were remodeled from a nineteenth century imitation Gothic to a very simple contemporary style. Graceful arches and stained glass windows gave way to stark simplicity: straight lines, bare white walls, plain choir stalls, a simple sanctuary. Rigidity in the practice of silence softened. The number of monks has decreased from around 270 in the late 1950's to around 110 today. Many were sent to establish new foundations; others left during the activist 1960's when the monastic life seemed an anachronism.

In the midst of these changes Matthew began to make his presence felt in the Gethsemani community. Solemnly professed in June, 1962, he took on increasingly important responsibilities in the monastery. One of his jobs was that of Vocation Director. He wrote a little booklet for prospective monks called "Aspects of the Monastic Calling" in which he described Cistercian life.

He began with what he believed to be the most important element in monastic living. "A calling to the monastic life is a call first of all to prayer. Serious, deep, abiding prayer. Prayer is communication, the relation of a lover to the loved one. It is not so much a matter of words as of attitudes, a disposition of the heart and a frame of mind.

"A man who is beginning to wonder whether or not he should become a monk is a wise man if he makes the wonder a form of prayer. He is touching something very awesome, indeed, very terrible. He may get burned."

Matthew then described the commitments which the monk must make. Stability: "That means that he belongs to that monastery and will remain there as long as he lives." Celibacy: "a way of love. It is not through the physical body and sexual communion, but on the mystical and spiritual plane." Community: "It is through his community that the monk is in touch with the monastic charism and its discipline. By means of the community he comes to know the gift of God and how to respond to it."

Solitude: "Monks are lonely men. This does not make them particularly different, since most men are lonely. It is what they do with their loneliness that makes them somewhat different." Silence: "It is probably the greatest single factor in spiritual growth." Poverty: "to live in a simple style of life synonymous with plain living." Obedience: "One must learn somehow to take one's life in one's hands and place it in the hands of another."

The most significant point to monastic living, however, is the monk's relationship with Jesus. "The whole thing revolves around Christ and love for him. Christ is the beginning of the monk's day and its end. Christ is the point of the monastic life, its core and purpose.

Without Him it is just a pious exercise. With him it is a love affair without parallel this side of eternity."

Finally, Matthew descibed the kind of person who makes a good monk. "We like it if you can listen to music and play some. We like it if you notice rain, feel the wind, hear the birds, smell the soup. We like you to be aware, not asleep; alive not dead; in touch, not gone. You ought to have your moral life pretty well in hand by the time you are thinking of a monastery. Sudden conversions are all right, but their depth should be tested."

Matthew held other responsibilities at Gethsemani. He was spiritual director for the lay brothers and, later, for the juniors, those who had completed the novitiate but had not taken final vows. He was sub-prior, he worked in the monastery shoe shop, and he was the first editor of *Monastic Exchange*, a quarterly journal that circulates among the Trappist houses.

He was happy in his new life. He found his place in the community rather quickly, his talents were appreciated, and he was given major responsibilities. Although the exterior of the abbey has a somewhat grim appearance due to the gray stone walls, it is a beautiful place as anyone who has spent a few days there knows. The little tree covered Kentucky hills or "knobs" as the monks call them, the rolling farm land, and the woods with their variety of wild flowers and vegetation are a perfect setting for contemplation. The quiet in the church is almost overwhelming. The mood created by the monotonous but stately chant of the monks during the Divine Office carries the human spirit to the heights and depths of religious feeling. One cannot escape believing that this is indeed the house of God and the gate of heaven.

Those who are intimately acquainted with monasteries know that the same human problems exist inside the cloister walls that are to be found in the world outside. Personality conflicts, jealousies, and hostilities are inevitable. Human weakness is not always left behind in the world. Yet, one senses at Gethsemani a spirit of calm and gentleness among the monks that is in sharp contrast to the aggression, anxiety, and hostility frequently encountered in the world.

Still, for Matthew, the normal monastic existence and regimen did not completely satisfy. A deep longing for God gripped him and remained unfulfilled. He remembered the loneliness of New Guinea which had been such a problem for him. Now, from a distance of over fifteen years it began to appear more attractive.

In the mid-1960's he began to live as a part time hermit. A small pump house in the woods below a dam on one of the Abbey ponds became a hermitage. He was given permission to spend most mornings there, overnight Sunday, and all day Monday. He spent the time in quiet, usually reading, playing a flute or guitar, practicing simple prayer, and doing a little yoga. Once a week he said Mass. He enjoyed the surrounding woods, the lake, and all of the features of the environment that produced a natural quiet and calm.

Matthew confessed, however, that even this partial solitary life was not easy. He wrote in his journal, "There are times when it is all I can do to go out there. There is some strange power that frightens me and makes me want to beg off, for I fear it. I always go and in the end I find that going out to meet it drives it away."

There was nothing easy about solitude. "There are things a monk must wrestle with. There are no doubt demons in the desert. To deny that is foolhardy in the extreme. But on the other hand, we are not to be frightened by them. We have Christ and the saints and the holy angels."

Matthew believed that environment is a major influence on how people live and think about themselves. In the same journal entry he wrote, "There are perhaps facets to my character and yours which would surprise both you and me if we were to live in a concentration camp for two or three years. I experience myself as almost another person when in community and when alone in the woods. No doubt we are one thing in the monastery and another out of it."

One of his continuing theological interests was the problem of evil. An obvious manifestation of evil is war, and there would develop within Matthew a growing concern about war, especially in Viet Nam. Evil is a mystery, he believed. In the monastic life it could be muted or even coaxed to be dormant. But it was there, and in the solitary life one was forced to face it and come to terms with it. This seemed to be one of Matthew's major reasons for seeking the hermit life. "We need to plunge into our own depths now and then," he wrote. "We need this contact with darkness."

Solitude, he knew, would not solve the problem of evil for anyone, but it would provide the opportunity to wrestle with it. And he concluded this section of his journal, "For having met evil in your own heart, you go out and stand under the sky. You listen to the chirping of the birds as you throw some bread crumbs to them. The sun is bright on the snow. The pines are rich against the cold sky and you wonder why it is. The sun warms your skin, as it warms the cold earth and all the things that sleep in it till Spring and you try to fathom the strange mystery of evil. I do not have an answer. I am only saying that you had better reckon with it."

The visits to the pump house were very helpful for Matthew, but at best this was only part time eremiticism. A desire for more was building within him. Thomas Merton had spent the last few years of his life as a hermit on Gethsemani property and was a strong influence. Dom James Fox, who retired as abbot in the late 1960's, went out into the woods to live the rest of his life as a solitary. His successor as abbot also had a strong interest in the hermit life. There were plentiful examples of the life of solitude at Gethsemani.

Rather than submit immediately to the desire to live alone, Matthew decided to wait until he had been at Gethsemani for ten years before making any attempt to seek it permanently.

The tenth year was 1969; it was time to explore the possibilities. He wrote to friends and other hermits he had heard about asking for advice. As the responses began to come in he saw three possibilities developing: Ireland, Canada, and New Guinea.

Ireland, he was told by a monk there, probably would not work out very well. The Irish had no real understanding of the hermit life, and the people would find a recluse such a curiosity that there would be much gossip and many problems. Furthermore, Matthew would be required to place himself under a bishop, and that might cause some difficulties.

A small community of hermits in Canada looked promising, but Matthew learned that it was going through major changes in structure and organization and had decided not to admit any new members for a while.

An enquiry to Papua New Guinea, however, produced the hoped response. Archbishop A. A. Noser, a member of the SVD whom Matthew had known in his missionary days, wrote back inviting him to come. The Archbishop had long wanted a contemplative community to settle in his diocese and believed that a monastic witness would strengthen the mission work there.

He suggested several places Matthew might live. No apostolic work would be required. The Archbishop simply wanted Matthew to live the Trappist life and promised to support him in every way, including financially. He warned Matthew that there would be no electricity, no running water, no hot showers, no modern conveniences. But the situation would be ideal for a hermit.

This invitation appealed to Matthew so much that he could scarcely contain himself. He began to write friends, literally all over the world, to ask for their opinions on a move to New Guinea. Most supported him, although some felt that the move was contrary to his personality and nature.

The next step was to begin the delicate process of negotiation with the Gethsemani community, and, specifically, the abbot, for permission to go. That process would take nearly five years.

In early talks with the abbot, Matthew stressed that his desire for solitude was a call from God to which he felt compelled to respond. He hoped it would be seen as a grace for Gethsemani as well as for himself, and believed that it would be a source of encouragement for the young monks. In response, Matthew was told that he was needed at Gethsemani. It is difficult for any community to give up someone who contributes leadership. But Matthew asked his abbot if his not being needed would ever come about?

Throughout these discussions Matthew insisted that he had no complaints about life at Gethsemani. He was happy there, he loved his brothers and found more than he had expected when he first entered. Still, this call to solitude overrode his love for community life. He told his brothers that he had not forgotten how difficult loneliness had been for him in New Guinea. He had been unprepared for it and it had been a terrible burden. But now his feelings about solitude had changed completely. "The thing has flipped on me. The thing I feared I have come to love," he said.

Matthew could easily have taken an option used by others. He would simply leave the Cistercian Order and go out on his own. It had been done by others at Gethsemani before him. The few juridical problems could have been overcome. But he refused to move under those circumstances. He wished to remain a monk of Gethsemani and would not go unless he had the blessing of his abbot and his community.

Continuing discussions with the abbot and other friends began to produce more objections to his leaving. To the argument that Gethsemani needed him, Matthew countered with the statement that the community must give in to the will of God. Monasteries expected others to make sacrifices for them; should not they be willing to make sacrifices themselves when a brother is called by God to solitude?

Matthew saw the whole affair as a matter of his own personal growth. "To go from a monastery into a greater kind of seclusion is not a freak adventure, but a healthy thing," he said. Indeed, the sixth century Rule of St. Benedict which governs Cistercian life provided for that very development. In Chapter 1 of the Rule, Benedict described hermits as those who "have served a mature probation in monasteries, and there learnt by the example and help of their fellow monks how to fight the devil; and thereafter are sufficiently appointed, without any other help than that of God, to enter the wilderness and fight a single combat against the sins of the flesh and the ill thoughts of the mind."

Matthew went through a good bit of intense self-examination during this period in his life. He was particularly interested in the role of male and female in an individual's life, a theme he would explore in more detail once he was in solitude. He had a feeling that his longing for the hermitage involved a desire to pull away from mother domination and to assert himself against the father. By mother he meant such forces as church, monastery, order, family, and religious community. Father was abbot, authority, rule, law, routine, system and organization. "I have long felt a need to detach myself from such a kind of dominance and meet the forces more from within," he told a friend. He did not see this as rebellion; in fact, he prided himself on having fit into monastic structures rather well. But he now sensed "a kind of obligation to test the certainty of my integration by standing alone before the Lord, in as dramatic a way as possible removed from the influence of both father and mother."

Not only did Matthew discuss the question of the solitary life with his community, but he carried on a lengthy correspondence with friends outside the cloister. Several of his former missionary associates encouraged him. They sensed that the mission enterprise was too much caught up in activity. In all of the good will and feverish zeal of missionary life the element of faith tended to get lost. In fact, Matthew was warned that missionaries, feeling such a strong need for spiritual renewal, would seek him out and his solitude would be lost.

While seeking reassurance from his friends that he was moving in the right direction Matthew still had some inner doubts. The remembrance of the New Guinea loneliness still haunted him. Although he now saw possibilities in it he had not seen at the time, he could not forget how hard it was. "I did not always find this a thing of delight," he wrote to a friend. "I found it very hard." He described his past relationship with solitude as "a rather uneven love-affair." He admitted that his desire for it now was ironic and was not what he had planned for himself when he first came to Gethsemani.

In a letter to an SVD priest he expressed his misgivings. "God knows I have fears of all kinds, fear of my salvation, my priestly and monastic vocation and what all. It may turn out a complete fiasco, a colossal joke. I may not be able to do it. I perhaps would be better off to do as a monk should do and stay in the monastery. And I try to tell myself this. But it does not work. I feel I am simply taking the easy way out when I do that, that I am betraying myself and the grace given me. So I will have to press the thing as hard as I can."

Matthew insisted that he went to Gethsemani because of a desire for God, and that it was in solitude where he was most aware of the divine Presence. It was, he confessed, a frightening Presence. Yet, it was a Presence that seemed to be drawing him inexorably into the hermitage. He often said that he did not see the solitary life as something secure, established, or even useful. For him, it was simply a matter of walking alone in faith.

After a few months of discussion with his superiors and others, Matthew began to feel resistance building up against his moving to New Guinea. He felt that the main argument used against him was that the monastic life is closed-ended; one must develop within the context of the community. Further, he was told that the kind of spiritual progress he hoped to make in solitude could be made within the walls of Gethsemani. Matthew was convinced that both of these points missed the main issue: what was God's will for him? He wanted to be obedient, but did not feel that the reasons given against his move to solitude were valid.

One realistic compromise would have been to let Matthew live as a hermit at Gethsemani. Merton had done it. Dom James Fox was doing it and, indeed, had invited Matthew to join him. But Matthew was not interested. "Let's face it," he said, "there is a romantic side to me and I simply need something a bit more exciting, a little bit more real." Being a hermit at the monastery was too safe. There were no risks. Moreover, and perhaps most important, Matthew felt that exile was an important dimension in solitude. "There is something to be said for leaving one's own land and people for the Lord. It would give some fiber to the solitude," he explained to a friend. Living in a primitive society in an underdeveloped country would have a sense of uncertainty about it that would make the whole venture a leap of faith. It would be like the desert fathers leaving the cities of ancient Egypt and going out into the wilderness to seek God.

Meanwhile, Archbishop Noser of New Guinea was keeping in touch. He told Matthew that opposition was to be expected. Doing the will of God often involves a cross. This may be a way of testing the validity of the request. As a good bishop he encouraged Matthew to accept the decisions of his superiors without question, but reminded him that if the call to solitude was indeed the will of God it would be worked out. At any rate, the invitation still stood if and when Matthew did receive permission.

By the middle of 1969 the negotiations were reaching a very delicate state. Matthew wrote in a letter, "I am not having much luck." Close friends were encouraging him, but those in authority insisted that he was badly needed at Gethsemani. He was not sure how to proceed. He did not want to push for a decision so hard that he would get a flat "No!" On the other hand, he seemed to be making no progress. There was nothing to do but live a normal monastic life and hope that God in his mercy would open some doors later. "I must work it out gently in the Spirit," Matthew said.

The frustration of indecision led Matthew to explore more deeply his reasons for wanting to go to New Guinea, and he began to bring up issues not mentioned before. His lively, outgoing, somewhat aggressive personality was not always universally appreciated in a community which treasured silence and calm. In the middle of 1969 he told his abbot that he was aware that he might be something of a problem in the community with his continued agitation of the solitude question. In fact, he admitted that throughout his life he had had a way of making some people uncomfortable without really meaning to do so. That being the case, would it not be better if he simply moved on to something else? This, in itself, he realized, was not sufficient reason to grant him permission to go, but added to his other reasons it might have some significance. "Being rather cowardly," he said, "I may need this spur!"

Another argument he raised had to do with the nature of the Cistercian life itself. The monastery's emphasis on silence, solitude, and seclusion had helped create within him a love for the hermit life. Why should a monastic order which operates in an environment where this kind of development can take place suddenly close the door to someone who wants to go deeper into solitude? He complained about those who strangle the monastic life and make it a terminal thing with no further prospect of development. He strongly opposed what he called "watering down the monastic life in order to give it mass appeal." There is a need to provide various forms of it according to the work of the Holy Spirit within each individual. There is also a need, he said, for Gethsemani to be true to the spirit of Thomas Merton who saw the hermit life as legitimate within the Cistercian Order. It was in this context, as a monk in a Cistercian monastery, that Matthew wished to enter solitude.

Still making no progress in convincing his superiors, he suggested an alternative. Why could there not be organized a loose federation of hermits as a part of the Cistercian Order? Most Cistercians who had opted for the solitary life had to leave the Order. Yet several monasteries were experimenting with small "primitive foundations" where a few monks, three or four, would live a simple life together. Why not treat hermits the same way? By being a part of the Order they would be more closely related to the Church. Perhaps they could have their own novitiate in a regular monastery before going out on their own.

Suppose, Matthew suggested, that such a group went to New Guinea. The hermits would be a part of the Order, have a definite juridical relationship with it and, perhaps, have a Father Immediate to oversee them and serve as a liaison with the Order. Once there, however, they would live separately, following a very general "rule of life", but otherwise supporting themselves and developing their own pattern of life in work, prayer, reading, and other monastic duties.

Interestingly enough, Matthew's abbot had a strong inclination toward the solitary life and, a few years later, would resign his position to live as a hermit at Gethsemani. Ironically, Matthew felt that he should not even consider solitude, but should devote himself to leading the monastery.

By the Fall of 1969 Matthew was still corresponding and talking with friends about going to New Guinea. He noted that the argument that he was needed at Gethsemani was the kind of problem he had faced throughout his career. When he wanted to join the SVD his home pastor insisted that he become a priest in the local diocese. When the SVD was ready to send him to New Guinea some people said that he was needed in the United States. When he left New Guinea to come back to edit the mission magazine some said he was still needed on the field. And when he left the SVD to enter Gethsemani there was someone around to say that he was needed in mission work. Now that he wanted to go to New Guinea, many people were telling him that he was needed at Gethsemani. That seemed to be the strongest argument used against him.

One of the men for whom Matthew had the deepest respect was Dom James Fox, former abbot of Gethsemani, who had retired to a hermitage in the late 1960's. Naturally, he was sympathetic with Matthew's desire for solitude, but not with the idea of going to New Guinea. He warned Matthew that his solitude would be constantly invaded. He would have to go to town for supplies, people would find out about him and visit, he would be asked to give pastoral and spiritual care, and the former abbot knew that Matthew's generous spirit would not allow him to refuse.

Dom James offered to have Matthew join him where he lived. Here he would have the protection of Gethsemani, his supplies would be brought to him, and he would have much more genuine solitude than he would find in New Guinea. But this did not appeal to Matthew.

He wanted exile from his normal surroundings and the adventure of striking out on his own.

He wrote to Dom James, ". . . the romantic and poetic side of me needs to do it this wild sort of way. I know the country, the people, the situation, and — most of all — the Archbishop." On the matter of his solitude being disturbed he said, "The thing could be controlled: I could always move further in, or further down, or further up! It is a big country! And it must be said, because I have experienced it, that there is an impact to solitude in exile and in a primitive country with a stone age culture that simply cannot be had by just moving a few miles away from the abbey! That is why it appeals to me so."

An important element in Matthew's quest for solitude was the desire to find his own true self, his archetype as Jung called it. It was a search for identity, for that image of God which is in every person. To find it, he believed, one must go into the desert where there is nothing but the individual and God, where reputation, talents, status and possessions mean absolutely nothing. Here there would be no supportive community. Life would be stripped naked.

By the Fall of 1969 discussions had reached the point where Matthew felt that he could go to New Guinea, but the abbot still did not think it was the right move. In short, he would not be prevented from going, but if he went it would be without the full blessing and support of the community. Matthew felt that there was no objection to solitude itself, just the fear that he would soon find himself involved in a variety of pastoral and apostolic activities and his monastic vocation would be destroyed.

Since this seemed to be the most he could hope for Matthew planned to write Archbishop Noser and announce that he was coming, hopefully by next Spring.

He also had to see about giving up the editorship of *Monastic Exchange*. He was disappointed that Gethsemani was not more enthusiastic about the venture, but believed that there was a calling from God he could not resist. It was, he believed, a work of grace. He described the planned move as "a very difficult thing to do." It meant withdrawal from obedience to the abbot and becoming a part of the diocese of New Guinea. That was not an easy decision for a Cistercian monk of ten years to make. So, he would enter solitude in real poverty, stripped even of the support of his community.

Matthew made the decision in his mind, but he had not, in fact, made it in his heart. He made a few more protests that the abbot should give him his blessing. He complained that the abbot would not give him a firm yes or no, but would simply say that it was Matthew's decision. Matthew wanted to be obedient. A firm "no" would have been better than a tolerant "you do what you wish."

Within a week Matthew had changed his mind. He posted a card on the monastery bulletin board announcing that he and the abbot had decided that it would be best if he not go to New Guinea. He would continue his duties as editor of *Monastic Exchange* for the next year. He would live in the faith that if the solitary vocation was indeed the will of God for him, God would find some way to provide it. He could not at this time bring himself to leave the Order and he realized that this would be required for him to go to New Guinea.

But he did not give up the idea of the hermit life. Even after making the decision he was still very disappointed and did not understand why he could not go. He complained in a letter of "being strangled and smothered by a force I cannot understand."

Archbishop Noser wrote to comfort Matthew, telling him that it is through those in authority that God reveals his will. Divine Providence, he said, often acts in unexpected ways. The defeat of the cross produced the triumph of redemption. The Archbishop provided Matthew with much needed pastoral care, counseling patience and trust in the work of the Holy Spirit. Never once did he encourage any disobedience, but, on the other hand, he was ready to support Matthew whenever permission to enter the hermitage might be granted.

II.
Oxford

Thirty miles north of Durham, North Carolina, a city famous for Duke University and tobacco industries, lies the little town of Oxford. Typical of many eastern North Carolina communities it was once dominated by its tobacco market but is now beginning to industrialize. Its main streets are lined with large trees and old stately houses, giving it the standard appearance of countless other small southern towns. During the 1960's it went through the same racial traumas other places in the south experienced. Its history was marred by one particularly unhappy incident in which a black youth was shot by a white policeman. Demonstrations, violence, and bad feelings followed. The Ku Klux Klan became active and still has signs posted around the county. But, like many other places in the South, Oxford has moved beyond those days. Things are reasonably peaceful and the 7,100 inhabitants have accepted change and have learned to live with it.

Five miles north of Oxford, near what is called the Lewis Community, once lay the sprawling Chewning plantation. Before the Civil War slaves farmed the land. In more recent times Martha Chewning, who lived on what was left of the plantation, converted to Roman Catholicism. She was eighty years old at the time and she became a member of the parish in Henderson, a town seventeen miles to the north. In her will she left her land to the Diocese of Raleigh. Challenges by heirs ultimately reduced the gift to less than thirty acres.

Nothing was done with the land for almost a quarter of a century. Bishop Vincent Waters of Raleigh had long wanted a monastic community in his diocese, but it was not until 1964 that he was able to arrange for one. In that year Father Peter Minard, a French Benedictine monk, arrived to found a monastery on the Chewning land. A small, slight man who radiated love and religious devotion, Father Peter labored for over five years to establish the monastery and put it on a firm foundation.

The first building was a double wide mobile home which, by the way, he first refused to live in because he felt it was too plush. Monks have since named it the Martha Chewning House. Father Peter knew how to raise money and eventually contracted to have the main buildings of the monastery erected. A simple wooden chapel was blessed on November 11, 1968. A large L-shaped building, also of frame construction, housed the library, kitchen, dining room, bathroom, and guest rooms. The library is outstanding for such a small monastery. It houses several thousand volumes, mostly on theology and monastic history, but also includes books on carpentry, organic gardening, and other practical subjects essential for survival.

Small wooden cabins, approximately ten feet square, were built for each of the monks. These cabins are plain and simple, reflecting the kind of life Father Peter hoped would be lived there. A larger building which serves as a tool house and workshop completes the layout.

Father Peter was interested in the surrounding community and involved himself in its life. He spoke to groups, raised money, and was particularly concerned with racial matters. He believed that a racially integrated monastery would be a good witness in eastern North Carolina, but that was a dream never fulfilled.

The monks who helped him begin soon left. Young people in the area were attracted to Father Peter and frequently visited him, but no one came to live permanently. By 1969 Father Peter had discovered that he was a victim of leukemia. Knowing he could not carry on he returned to France to live out the rest of his life as a hermit.

Fortunately, Father Peter found other Benedictines interested in Oxford who agreed to take over when he left. A small group led by Father Claude Peiffer arrived in 1969. Father Claude is a scholar and author of a fine book, *Monastic Spirituality*, as well as other writings. However, the rustic nature of the Oxford monastery proved unsuitable to the style of the group, and in a few months it was obvious these monks would have to move elsewhere.

In the hope of finding new residents for the monastery inquiries were made to a number of religious communities, including the Abbey of Gethsemani. The abbot there was personally interested in the solitary life and in small experimental communities where the monastic life could be lived without the burden of maintaining a large abbey. He hoped that Gethsemani would experiment in this direction and began to look for a few monks willing to move to Oxford. One of the first people he approached was a monk who had been asking for permission to live as a hermit, Matthew Kelty. Matthew and another monk were dispatched to North Carolina to look the situation over and bring back an evaluation.

At first glance there is nothing particularly beautiful about the Oxford site. The soil is red clay. The woods are mostly pine trees. There is a one and a half acre tobacco field. Other parts of the land are bare with patches of clay and grass. The property does not front any road and access to it is by a very bad lane that is almost impassable in bad weather. The white mobile home reflects much of the ugliness of a prefabricated society, and the wooden buildings are utilitarian and unattractive. Still, after one has been there for a while the place has a certain charm and peacefulness.

Matthew and his brother monk spent a few days and returned to Gethsemani to report. The brother was somewhat less enthusiastic about the project than Matthew, but believed it to be a viable situation. It was, he thought, well suited to the type of experimentation in which the abbot was interested. He felt that at least four monks should live there in order that maintenance and housekeeping not become such burdens that they distract the monks from their prayer. He recommended that several monks move to Oxford and try it for a year or two.

For Matthew's part, he had never been very enthusiastic about small group monastic living. In a little piece he wrote in 1967 he said, "While there can be no doubt that some kind of monastic life can be had with a small and intimate group living in rugged conditions, I do not accept as proven that this is best, the ideal, the Cistercian way, or, finally, the one best suited to our times. On the contrary, I would maintain that on the basis of history and experience that the facilities necessary for the monastic life in some depth are considerable and are best provided for when the group is relatively large."

His report to Gethsemani on Oxford was rather negative. "If I myself were looking simply for a hermitage or a place for a life of solitude, I would want it, I think, to be somewhat romantic, picturesque, even dramatic and wild. Oxford is not like that. There is no sea or lake or river nearby or on the property. There are no mountains or even hills; it is almost perfectly level. It is a relatively poor country."

Still, he saw possibilities there. "Oxford would give more scope to private and personal prayer in a more quiet and a less active setting. This is not necessarily a better prayer or a more perfect prayer, but it is a prayer to which some are called."

Even on a brief visit Matthew was able to sense what would be one of the biggest problems for most monks who went there. "I feel that the best thing about Oxford will also be the worst: that is to say, solitude. I believe the place very lonely. Not all like loneliness this much or feel called to it. I feel that many might find the lonely quality of the area quite overpowering and would soon feel trapped or closed in. But for some, such solitude is a great grace and a road to deep prayer. To open the way to such a development, to experiment to see whether or not this can be fitted into the Cistercian way of life, seems to me something worthy of Gethsemani and a kind of leadership which we are called to and which others expect of us."

Matthew was willing to lead the experiment. He made it plain to the abbot that his real desire was to go to New Guinea and live as a hermit. But, if that was not possible he would be an obedient monk and go to Oxford.

On June 24, 1970, the feast day of John the Baptist, Matthew and two brothers from Gethsemani arrived at the little monastery. They hoped to support themselves by weaving, in which they would soon receive instruction, and would try to prove that the contemplative life could be lived successfully in a small setting. Although they were the third group of monks to occupy the place, which now was called the Monastery of the Holy Mother of God, they were the first Trappists.

In a few months they had developed a document called "Some Tentative Norms," a set of guidelines which regulated their daily existence. It was obvious that elaborate liturgy would not work at Oxford. Something other than the Gethsemani style of worship would have to do. The monks decided on three Divine Offices each day. Vigils would be at 3:00 A.M., Lauds at 6:00 A.M., and Vespers at 6:00 P.M. At each office the men would take turns reading psalms, and the whole psalter would be covered in a week. In addition, at Vigils a portion of the Old Testament would be read, at Lauds a section from the Gospels, and at Vespers a reading from the rest of the New Testament. Each office would end with the Lord's Prayer and the Hail Mary. It was all very simple: scripture and silence. Following Lauds each morning Matthew would offer Mass.

The monks observed silence most of the time. The one common meal would be at noon, and there they would talk over anything that needed discussion. The men were expected to work about four hours each day, usually in the morning. In the afternoons they would try to keep out of each other's way and spend that time in reading and prayer. Although the monastery had about $13,000 in the bank left over from the previous occupants, Matthew felt that the monks should have to work for a living like anyone else. "To make something useful with one's hands, sell it for a fair price, and keep the whole thing cool and quiet is what we like."

The layout of the monastery buildings made the traditional monastic enclosures impossible. There were no walls behind which the monks could retreat from the world. No gatehouse inhibited visitors. So, the usual strictness about avoiding the world simply had to be dropped. The procurement of supplies and other practical necessities required trips into Oxford. The "Tentative Norms" stated, "We go to town only when we must. When we do we enjoy it and talk to people for the simple reason that we love them. But we still prefer the dialogue that goes on in the woods." Solitude, said Matthew, has its difficulties and tensions, but the monks know they have to endure them "if the fruit is to be tasted."

Living in a small community, close together, was bound to produce occasional conflicts. There were disagreements, especially in the early days of trying to work out the procedures and style of the community. The "Tentative Norms" warned that "hidden resentments and unspoken hostilities are to be avoided, since if they do not come out in the normal way (talking them out) they will come out in some abnormal way (headaches, indigestion). We must try to live a peace that is real, not a pious fraud. Being demure in the world pays, for it is good business. But this is not our way. Our peace is to be real. Better an honest fight loud and clear, than a burning fire hidden by a sweet face." The poverty of the community was not just economic, it also involved shortcomings and faults of character.

In all of the traditions, rules, practices, and observances of the monk's existence the real purpose of his life, to deepen the individual's relationship with Christ, is sometimes forgotten. Matthew described the monastery at Oxford as "a commune with a singular devotion to the person of Jesus Christ, and this gives it a very specific and special character. He is the point of the place and life revolves around Him."

For Matthew, one of the major characteristics of the Oxford monastery was freedom. "This is a place of freedom and a place for freemen. If there is one basic requirement for the monk coming here, it is that he must be free. If he is hung up on half a dozen things that he 'must have,' or 'absolutely needs,' then he is not a free man." The life at Oxford was a disciplined life, and discipline, said Matthew, makes one unselfish. Unselfishness is a characteristic of the free man. "Hence," he said, "we seek to go through the day easily and in peace, without fear and anxiety. And yet with an order and peace that makes the place move along the way a good athlete, as a good dancer, can play a good game, do a happy dance, which at once is nice to look at and a joy to see, but also done easily and even merrily. Good athletes, like good dancers, are disciplined."

Matthew and his two brothers settled into the Oxford life, developing a routine of simple living. No radio or television distracted them, no complex regulations. The first few months they occasionally wore simple gray habits left by previous occupants, but finally discarded them as unnecessary. Except for the traditional white cowls worn only in chapel, they dressed in plain work clothes. In outward appearance they were no different from any other Granville county workers.

After nine months, a gestation period, Matthew returned to Gethsemani to report on the progress at Oxford. He admitted that one reason he came back to Gethsemani was homesickness. "There is no place on earth that turns me on the way this place does." He also felt a need to get away from Oxford for a few days in order to get a better perspective on it.

Matthew reminded his brothers that his strongest desire was for solitude. He had asked for permission to live as a hermit, had been refused, and in monastic obedience had accepted the decision. But, the desire was still there. In the aftermath of that controversy the Oxford experiment had presented itself. He had gone, forcing as much enthusiasm as he could, but he told his brothers, "My mind is not wholly clear on Oxford. I have never thought of it as my place and what is going on there as Matthew's thing." But he said that he agreed with the abbot that Oxford-like communities could well be the style of monasticism in the future. Since Oxford was there, paid for, and ready for occupancy, it was worth a try. If the experiment failed, nothing much was lost.

Those who visited Oxford while Matthew was there saw him express considerably more enthusiasm for the project. Perhaps it was because we did not know about the New Guinea situation until near the end of his stay. He never talked about it. But, one was always impressed with the way Matthew showed people around the buildings. He fairly danced, his eyes shone, and as far as any one could tell, he was ecstatically happy to be there.

In his report at Gethsemani Matthew noticed that there were only a dozen Catholic families in Oxford. The local priest served three parishes from a home base in Henderson. Matthew asked for, and would later receive, a grant of money from Gethsemani to help reduce the indebtedness on the Oxford Catholic Church.

In describing the little monastery to his brothers Matthew mentioned the noise problem. There was a large population of dogs in the neighborhood whose barking could be heard all night. Passing automobiles, trucks, and airplanes constantly disturbed monastic silence. "But," he said, 'when you live there the noise seems little and there is a certain comfort in it."

Another problem was loneliness. The monastery was slightly inaccessible, and a week might go by without a phone call or a visitor. That would change in the future. One of Matthew's problems during his last two years at Oxford was a steady influx of visitors, particularly college students and young people.

One of his main concerns was the racial situation in the area. The Oxford establishment was determined to maintain the old Southern life style as long as possible. Matthew respected the people of the area. "They are just like the people down Maine I knew as a boy when I went there summers: frugal, plain living, good family people, pious, decent, honest, good citizens, and very narrow. The southern version simply adds a kind of contempt for the blacks which puts them in their place and keeps them there."

Matthew wanted the monastery identified with the plight of blacks in the Oxford area. To this end he secured another grant of money from Gethsemani for the local black orphanage. The grant was publicized in the local paper. As a matter of fact, the racial situation improved more rapidly than Matthew anticipated, but during his first year there were violence, burnings, and other disorders.

He also worried about the poverty in the county, some of which was in evidence right next to the monastery property. He believed that monks should make some kind of witness in the situation. They did not have to engage in an active apostolate, but neither should they appear to sit idly by and condone the situation. "If we end up doing nothing because we are men of prayer who live in seclusion, we may for all practical purposes look exactly like the white establishment who also do nothing, though for different reasons."

Blacks did visit the monastery occasionally, as they had done during Father Peter's day. He had been told by the locals that interracial visiting was not the custom, but he ignored them and experienced no trouble other than having the monastery sign burned one night. The blacks who came by for a visit expressed appreciation for the monastery and did not necessarily see it as an agency of social change. One elderly black man who had been a tenant of Martha Chewning told Matthew that monks are like John the Baptist. They go into the desert, stay there, and meditate. That had particular meaning for Matthew since he had begun his stay at Oxford on the feast day of John the Baptist.

In his talk at Gethsemani he reemphasized the loneliness of the life at Oxford. "We are not solitaries or hermits, but it is a lonely life and a life of quiet is hard. So little is going on that really all there is is the interior. There is nothing else." But loneliness had its advantages. "In a quiet life there is an experience of God that for those called to it is not had in any other way. By experience of God I do not mean some dramatic encounter as much as a growth in knowledge and love. Plenty have come and seen what was there and have got the point of it and told me very frankly that they were much pleased and hoped for blessing on it."

During the period of Gethsemani's sponsorship Oxford was always tentative; its future uncertain. No one in Kentucky was particularly interested in it other than the abbot. "The whole project in Oxford is very fragile and little, a frail thing," Matthew said. "This makes a man turn to God and put himself in His hands." But, he believed that there was some sort of Divine Providence at work. Why did Martha Chewning convert to Catholicism in the last years of her life? Why did she give land to the diocese? Why was the land kept idle until Father Peter built a monastery only to leave it to others, the Benedictines, and, finally, the Trappists, "only in the end for us to come, men of no great pretensions and of modest stature to be perhaps what God had in mind from the beginning?"

Matthew concluded his report with an admonition that has characterized much of his life and writing. "My brothers, you have to be real careful with God. You have to be careful you do not buck him or resist Him. It is so easy to do and it is easiest of all to do it for the best of reasons. I do not pretend to know His will; I do not pretend to know His will for Oxford. All I say is that you have to play it cool and you have to stay free. You have to hold your hand out and let Him take whatever is on it and let Him place there whatever He has in mind. After all, everything we have is from Him and to Him we have to offer everything we have. This is a good song to sing."

Matthew returned to Oxford and immersed himself in it. The two brothers who had accompanied him from Gethsemani eventually left. Oxford was just not their style. Each went his own way, but each eventually found his way back to Gethsemani. A monk from an abbey in the northeast came and stayed almost two years. He seemed to like the life and had a genuine mystical spirit. But eventually he too left, and entered a monastery in the west. Another brother from Gethsemani arrived at Oxford to help Matthew during his last few months there and is now in a monastery in New York state. Others came for short stays. There were frequent retreatants and several tried the life with a view to entering another house if they were able to adjust. But no one would stay permanently.

The life at Oxford was very hard. There were none of

the supports found in large abbeys: beautiful architecture, good music, solemn habits, and much activity. One of the monks said to me, "Some people can't get used to the fact that nothing ever happens around here." For a deeply formed monk this is an advantage; for one less fully developed in Trappist life it causes boredom and restlessness.

Toward the end of his stay Matthew told me that no one would settle permanently as long as he was in charge. Did he feel that his personality was a problem for people, or was his insistence on a particular way of living a deterrent? Neither, probably. There was nothing at Oxford but God, and most people simply cannot stand that. The contemplation of God drives some people to despair, and their only hope is that some distraction will keep them from having to face up to their own poverty and lack of spiritual attainment.

As people became better acquainted with the monastery Matthew's volume of correspondence increased. This prompted him to duplicate an occasional newsletter which he would send to his friends, reporting on the progress of the community and his own personal feelings about things.

In an issue dated "Early Summer 1972" he reported on the population of the monastery. There were now two monks: Matthew and a priest from a monastery in New England. In addition, a teaching brother from Massachusetts was there for the summer, investigating the possibilities of the Trappist life for himself. He did enter Gethsemani, but eventually decided that teaching was his real vocation. Another temporary resident was a deacon from Portugal. Other residents included three goats (Philip Morris, Phyllis, and Miranda), a dog, a cat, eight guinea hens, and two peacocks. Matthew also reported that a number of guests had dropped by, especially college students "what with school getting out." A young woman active in the peace movement also appeared for a visit. Matthew said that she "made a profound impression on us. If this is the Catholic left, you may call me their friend."

There was an ominous note in the letter. "When we heard that our abbot may resign come Fall we got a bit dizzy for a moment, just for a passing moment. When you sail a small craft like this, you learn early to keep your eye on the water." Matthew did not know that this forthcoming resignation would finally make it possible for him to go to New Guinea. For the moment, the uncertainty about the future of Oxford was his main concern.

Matthew joined the Carolina Designer Craftsmen after having submitted some of his work for approval. This led him to take his loom to Raleigh for a craft show. His sister came down from Massachusetts to serve as hostess in his booth, and he wove for two full days. The show enabled him to make some good outlet contacts for his work. Such a trip was not a normal monastic procedure, and Matthew found it exhausting, but his innate love for people was satisfied. "I thought the arts and crafts people would be somewhat weirdy," he wrote, "but it turns out they are not such: good bunch, real likeable; you might say they are just like us, a most respectable people!"

Another item of interest in the newsletter was a report on his Honda motorbike, a beloved if non-monastic possession. It was his favorite mode of transportation. "On a bike you are out in the air, the wind, the weather. I have ridden in twenty degree weather, in pouring rainstorms, in the night, and think it is a marvelous way to ride. Only danger is you get carried away into mystic flights and that is bad; you have to keep your mind on what you are doing and mind the beauty too. Did you know people treat you differently when you ride a bike? Much more friendly. And if you think it's only hoodlums and young ones who ride, you are mistaken."

This newsletter revealed a fact often surprising to lay people: monks are usually rather well informed on what is going on in the world. Matthew did not ignore politics. "I registered locally and thus am able to vote here. This area was for Wallace in the primaries. I wasn't."

Out in the world the war in Vietnam was continuing, and Matthew was deeply troubled by it. Peace posters began to appear on the monastery buildings. To the unhappiness of the local bishop Matthew had the telephone removed. He could not stop the war but he could refuse to pay the federal tax on phone calls. In the newsletter he said that the shrieks of the monastery peacocks in the night reminded him of the screaming children of Viet Nam. He expressed a desire to make some kind of witness for peace and said that he might walk to Washington, D.C. as a "protest pilgrimage for peace." But he did not know how appropriate that would be for a monk. The peace visitor had had an influence.

After weeks of wrestling with the idea and discussing it with friends Matthew did decide to walk to Washington as pilgrimage and protest against the war. He chose August 6, 1972, as his departure day. It was the feast of the Transfiguration and the twenty-seventh anniversary of the atomic bombing of Hiroshima. It was also the day when fourteen people in the peace movement in New York would begin a forty day fast for peace. One member of that group had visited Oxford earlier.

Around the first of August Matthew sent out another newsletter to his friends asking for support. "This nation was born of a violent revolution; we have walked the path of violence ever since. We now hover on the brink of a total disaster as men of war, drunk with power, tinker with weapons resembling the power of Almighty God in their capacity to blot out all the creation we know. How long now voices have been raised for peace and with no apparent result whatever. Still, it is important not to lose heart, to carry on. That being so, it seemed singularly appropriate for me to do something, however pathetic, however tardy, for the cause of peace."

He asked his friends to pray for him that "1) I may be able to make the whole walk (it is about 235 miles and I am 56), 2) that it may do some good, and 3) that the Oxford monastery may escape a lot of publicity and curious people."

His destination would be the Shrine of the Immaculate Conception in Washington. He planned to enter it wearing a cowl that had once belonged to Thomas Merton who had written much on peace. Matthew had been his confessor. Then he would say Mass.

After a midnight Mass at the monastery, Matthew set out on his journey in the early hours of August 6, accompanied by the monastery dog, Polka. People in the peace movement wanted to publicize the walk and some news releases were sent out by them. Stories on the departure and return appeared in the Raleigh, North Carolina *News and Observer* and the Oxford *Public Ledger*. A few other local papers along the route picked up the story.

The walk took twelve days. The first two nights were spent in a small tent, but it was soon discarded as too heavy. Rectories and motels provided lodging the rest of the way.

Needless to say, a public protest is not a normal kind of monastic, especially Trappist, activity, and Matthew received serious criticism from many of his fellow monks. Some refused to support him because he had not asked his abbot's permission. Many said that a monk's place is in his monastery. One monastery, however, sent around a statement asking monks to support Matthew during the time of his walk with prayer and fasting. A surprising number of monks signed and returned the printed statements to Matthew.

He made it as far as a cemetery in Washington and was met there by the peace movement people. The *National Catholic Reporter* ran a story and described his condition upon arrival. "The monk's face was red and peeling from the sun, setting off his whitish hair and bright blue eyes. He was in high spirits." After offering Mass at the altar of the Virgin of Guadalupe he spent a few days at the SVD house in Washington and visited a nearby Trappist community. Finally, friends drove him home. *Berryville, Va.*

Letters began to arrive at Oxford from all over the world. Some came from people in jail for their opposition to the war. For the most part the letters could be placed in three categories. First were those which expressed outright opposition to the walk. Some writers felt that Matthew had been unfair in his criticisms of his fellow monks for not doing more to stop the war. Second, there were a number of letters from people who sympathized with Matthew's feelings, but said that they themselves could never do such a thing. They felt that they had to work out the matter of peace interiorly, that it was a spiritual, not a political problem. Third, the largest number of letters were strong in their support. Some of these came from Trappist monks. Others came from members of the peace movement who had become discouraged. Matthew's walk had lifted their spirits.

Upon returning to Oxford Matthew wrote out his feelings about the walk in a newsletter which he titled, "Reflections on an Ambiguous Journey." After describing the physical aspects of the journey he turned to a discussion of his philosophy about it. "Though not lacking in belligerence and even violence, I still consider myself a man of peace and have done so all my life: as priest, missionary, and certainly as monk. I look on my whole life as a 'peace action.' Certainly the contemplative life is rooted in peace with one's self, with one's neighbor, with God. A peace action in the market place seems somewhat superfluous in that case. Still, peace is having a hard time these days and the more I thought about it, discussed it, the more necessary it seemed to me to say something out loud, as it were, as a monk, for the cause of peace. Just to let peace know that we are kin."

He insisted that it was an individual act. "I do not think of it as a Cistercian thing, nor a Gethsemani thing, even, for that matter, an Oxford thing. It was simply a monk saying something for peace in a way that seems to me not out of keeping with his basic life thrust. I felt a certain call of the spirit to respond to grace." Aware of the criticism that he did it without seeking permission, he responded. "I did not ask my abbot simply because I did not think it fair to do so; I saw no reason to hang the thing around his neck and make him carry it. It seemed to me within our competence, that we should assume responsibility for it."

There were some ambiguous elements in the pilgrimage. One day Matthew and his dog were attacked by a very large dog. Matthew had to kick him several times with his boot to drive him away. The contradiction of a man of peace engaging in violence against an animal could not be ignored. "I did a lot of thinking about it. But we deal with mystery. Violence is a mystery because it is rooted in evil somehow, in sin, our common heritage. And the evil influence floats around in us all. It needs little encouragement. Violence breeds violence. And that is why peace is rooted in prayer, in grace. We deal with something far greater, far deeper, than we realize. It is a kind of demon driven out only by prayer and fasting."

For Matthew it was a matter of "living it out as best we can. For if there are monsters in our depths, and there are, there is also the presence of God. And when we touch that, we set free the power of love. Love breeds love. Peace breeds peace."

Some leaders of the peace movement were discouraged that the war, at least the bombing, seemed to be getting worse. Matthew's walk encouraged them and, likewise, Matthew was impressed with them. He particularly appreciated the fact that these social activists understood what the monk's life is all about. "Certainly the monk's life is ambiguous; he does nothing, he works at the world's problems in the silence and solitude of the desert, a scandal to man. But it is a scandal that does not fool peace people. They are wise to monks. They are up to what we are doing. Party to it. They find in us brothers and kindred spirits."

He described Washington as "a loud noisy dirty city, a lot of frosting over a lot of burned cake. And in and out of it move lots of good people, holy people, serious and sincere people. They can use a little peace and quiet, a little prayer, a little love and hope."

Returning to Oxford he felt "much enriched, much deepened, but filled with worry and with foreboding. What lies ahead of us?" But the little monastery was a welcomed sight. "This place never looked as sweet and lovely as when I returned to it. It was never so welcome a sight, so radiant a vision. And when I walked into the library and saw there two turtle doves given by a friend while I was away, I was near tears. Two doves, white ones. They coo for peace. I call them Peace and Joy. What a beautiful gift. All day long they quietly speak for peace. And at dawn and at twilight. And in the dark of night the peacocks scream for help."

A few months later another newsletter went into the mails dated "Advent 1972." Its tone was melancholy, though not without hope. "I cannot decide whether the Monastery at the moment is enjoying an interlude, a low point or a high point. It seems to be something of all three." The interlude was caused by the fact that the abbot of Gethsemani had asked for permission to resign and return to the hermit life, and the monks there seemed willing for him to do it. This left the question of Oxford's future very much up in the air. A new abbot might not be interested in the project, but Matthew felt that "Oxford will carry on, and about as heretofore, but certainly the question of the resignation does constitute a kind of interlude for us here. A time for holding the breath. A sort of waiting quietly on the Lord."

The monastery was at a low point in that only one monk was there now: Matthew himself. At last he was a hermit. All monks and prospects had departed. "So I have the place to myself, save for a visitor now and then. And this I find sort of a high point, for it is a rather delightful time. I have not been here alone for any period up till now and I find the place to be something else again when by myself. I daresay I rather like it."

Even a small monastery like Oxford required a good bit of maintenance and housekeeping, and it was all really too much for one man. The weaving production dropped significantly. Still, said Matthew, "the overall quiet is very beautiful. Just as one is conscious of people when they are here, so I live conscious of peace and quiet and find they are as rich in message as people are, only of a different kind. The place is surely not empty."

The animal population declined as well. The chickens stopped laying, so Matthew gave them away. The goats were getting stingy with their milk; they were sent to a neighbor. The peacocks and guinea hens were still pecking around the monastery grounds, however.

After his peace walk Matthew tried a twenty day fast, taking only water and fruit juice. He found it better than the usual monastic fast in which one meal a day was eaten. By eating nothing "the digestive system more or less goes to sleep and then hunger disappears. This spares you the preoccupation with food fantasies all day, a likely thing with an empty stomach which is wide awake."

Toward the end of this newsletter Matthew wrote on a theme of great interest to him, one he would write about more when he finally became a hermit. The theme was the relationship of male and female within the individual. He reported on a meeting he had attended on small contemplative communities. "The most stimulating item that came up, for me anyway, as for others, was the notion of mixed communities of men and women." Such communities have never had any lasting success in traditional Christian monasticism, but the future, of course, need not be bound by the past. Matthew thought, "it would be a good thing to try." He proposed two separate groups, men and women, who would live their separate lives but share together in common prayer through the Divine Offices and the Eucharist. They might use a common library and perhaps join together for a meal on occasion. Man and woman can meet on many levels, and one of the most important is "the life of the Spirit, the search for God in the celibate state." He complained that our society was characterized by "an extreme divorce of man and woman: this has affected both parties, and has considerable repercussions in the life of prayer, the monastic life. A certain amount of contact, modified, disciplined, but real, might be a good thing." Matthew felt very strongly that there must be a union of male and female elements within each individual. He even saw that marriage as being "symbolic of the greater inner union that we are all called to."

He concluded the letter, "I expect to be alone into the New Year and look forward to it. It is a good way to prepare for His coming, this one and the final one. And in His coming day by day." Speaking more prophetically than he realized in the wake of the 1972 elections Matthew wrote, "I rather think we will much need Him these next four years."

Just a few months later, in February 1973, another newsletter began to circulate. This issue gave almost no information about Oxford, but was an essay on monastic obedience prompted by the arrival of an official notice that an election for a new abbot would be held at Gethsemani on March 15. It is evident that the desire to go to New Guinea had not lessened, and the disappointment over not being allowed to go was still being painfully borne.

The abbot had been a hermit before his election. According to Matthew, the hermit had asked him if he should accept the office if elected. Matthew replied that he should see such an election as the will of God. Five years later when the official visitor from the motherhouse in France asked Matthew if the abbot should be allowed to step down and return to the hermitage the reply was, "Yes. If the Spirit calls him to that we should show reverence to the Spirit." So, Matthew concluded, "I helped the man in and I helped the man out."

But what had the abbot done for him? Matthew had asked for for permission to live as a hermit in New Guinea and had been turned down by his superior. In spite of this disappointment, however, Matthew was able to keep things in perspective. "I promised to obey the man, and that promise was not qualified by a willingness to do so only when I thought he was right. God can work in any set of conditions." And, his own frustrations aside, Matthew affirmed, "Gethsemani liked him as abbot and he leaves a good aroma after him."

Perhaps the abbot's greatest contribution to Matthew's own life was in forcing him to face up to the issue of obedience. "Obedience is hard for monks. I think we fail here more than in any other area. Monks like to chide themselves for their lack of silence, of charity, of zeal for prayer, for lack of poverty. But I think it is in obedience that we fail most. It is very hard, that is why. To my mind, all the ascetic practices there are do not amount to much compared to the asceticism of obedience." Modern man, Matthew knew, finds obedience "a stern and unpopular master."

Reflecting on the life of Thomas Merton, his own novice master, Matthew noted that Merton worked very hard, but was no great ascetic. But Merton's abbot often said of him that there was never a more obedient monk. Matthew saw significance in that. "Through obedience he became a free man. And it is the free who love, who speak of victory."

It is by obedience that "we are set free of ego and the false self and attain to union with God, with the Lord Jesus." Everyone, said Matthew, is bound to obey God. Yet, God can come into people's lives in terrible ways. Witness the suffering that most people in the world endure. God is a mystery. "But this much I know," wrote Matthew, "as everyone knows who has looked up from his book a moment, that God is at times pretty terrible. Terrifying. Awesome. And people have to live with that, whether they know God or not, love him or not. And make do, somehow."

The monk simply enters into this mystery a little deeper than most other people. "Instead of waiting on God to come, he goes out to meet Him, in the desert, as it were. But God met in the desert is no different from God arriving suddenly and unannounced. Pretty awful. It is in the context of obedience that often enough this takes place."

And here, of course, Matthew was thinking about his hoped for life as a hermit. The hermitage is a desert. "After all," Matthew admitted, "you do not have to go out into the desert to meet God. He will come anyhow. But the point of going out is to enter more surely and more deeply into the human experience and by it open up the whole situation. The hermit is simply carrying the thing one step further and meets the Lord directly, without an abba, a father. This is obviously a great deal more difficult and dangerous."

Obedience, Matthew believed, can reveal the love of God at work. "The whole experience of obedience can lead one deep into a great compassion for the human family. It's a hard road that most mortals walk on their way into the kingdom, often enough with small comfort and little faith to sustain them on their arduous journey. The monk, if anyone, ought to have within him a profound grasp of the mercy of God and radiate it by his very being, for if he meets this hard God, he comes to know that He is not hard at all really; but all mercy." Behind all of the human misery and suffering in the world "somehow or other, God knows how, love is at work."

Matthew concluded the letter by wishing his retiring abbot well. "May he meet God. And if he finds God tough, and he will, he will also find God rich in mercy, which He is. And to know the mercy of God? That is everything."

Within a month there was another newsletter, this one headed "Thoughts after almost three years . . ." It was a reflection on life at Oxford and peoples' reactions to it. Looking back Matthew concluded, "I still feel that what we have here is very much a good thing and something there is a real need for. Though there has never been any doubt in my own mind that it is a good experience for monks and a valid form of the monastic life within the Cistercian ambit, it is in this last year or so that I have come to realize that it is also a great service to people who come in contact with it."

This is an unusual statement for a Trappist. Such monasteries are never founded to serve people on the outside, although hospitality has always been a part of the tradition. Still, visits to monasteries have increased in recent years. People interested in contemplative values have a way of finding them and they found Oxford. Reflecting his natural gregarious spirit Matthew wrote, "Far from being an intrusion and bother I have seen this as both stimulating and inspiring. For one thing, the problems are minor, since the guests simply enter into the life and do just as we do, taking part in the services in the chapel, sharing the common meal, working in the morning, quiet in the afternoon. It differs little from having monks around. Their grasp of what it is all about moves one deeply, their appreciation of what we have and what we stand for is a grace."

From personal experience I can attest to the genuineness of those reflections. He treated guests as if they were monks, putting them to work, but leaving them alone. Guests present when I was there always seemed to catch the spirit of the place and entered deeply into the silence and solitude. Those not inclined that way probably would not come around anyway.

Matthew wished that there were places like Oxford everywhere. "The people are so very hungry, so much in need of an experience of quiet, of simple worship, of a humble way of life which somehow is open to God. It is very touching. I am very much for seclusion and solitude and the hidden life and think a monk must have this. If he needs diversion and distraction the thing will not ring right. But when he's into what he's got, then sharing it in some modest way is no great problem."

Although alone at the time, Matthew wrote about his views on community life. "In a disintegrating society, how important community is, what a powerful expression of life and love! It is precisely for community that a great search goes on. But it takes a great deal of kenosis to build community, a lot of giving. Certainly, if each sets out to satisfy himself first of all, and sets the framework in which he finds his way to God, community will suffer. Something must express, after all, the fact that one has truly joined a community in a common quest for a life that will lead us to the perfect community in the kingdom."

Paradoxically, Matthew believed that only a good community man could succeed as a hermit. "No one should go into solitude who is not dearly in love with his brethren. He then sacrifices that love and takes the brethren with him in his heart and so enters even more deeply into the mystery of redemption. If the hermit does not have the whole wrapped in the love of his heart in God, he is no hermit but a man running away from love. That is why a good monastic community will always have real hermits: monks who have by reason of their monastic experience entered deeply into love of the human family, and having entered it, go off to dwell on that mystery alone. And there penetrate even more into the solidarity which is the human family redeemed and made one by the Lord Jesus."

In the newsletter Matthew mentioned the various guests that had appeared in recent months: college students, nuns, an Episcopal priest with the gift of healing, a young executive, a journalist, and others. I had been at Oxford a few months earlier making a retreat during the Christmas holidays. There was a fascinating group of people present. In addition to Matthew there was a psychologist from a nearby university, a Brooklyn policeman on his way to another monastery which he would ultimately enter, a member of the Little Brothers of Jesus who lived on the Bowery in New York, a young man looking for a religious community to join, and a hitchhiker on his way from Wisconsin to Alaska. Oxford was out of the way, but he had heard about it and wanted to visit for a few days.

Everyone entered right into the life. We each read our psalms during the offices, we cooked and washed dishes, we did menial jobs around the monastery, we read, we lived in silence, and we prayed. The only time for real talk was the noon meal and the conversation was stimulating to say the least. Matthew was the gracious host and the life of the party. But he was serious and gave us informal spiritual direction. I will always remember those three days with that beautiful collection of people.

Matthew ended the newsletter with the announcement that he would go to Gethsemani for the election of the abbot.

The abbot was chosen on March 15, 1973. Like his predecessor, he was one of the younger members of the community, though he was a thoroughly experienced monk. His brothers at Gethsemani described him as "a good community man." A few days after his election he wrote his first letter to Matthew saying that he was open to a new discussion about New Guinea. Matthew could hardly believe what he read. After years of frustration it now began to look as if his wishes would be fulfilled. The abbot promised to visit Oxford soon to discuss the matter. Meanwhile, another monk from Gethsemani would be sent to help Matthew. The Spring of 1973 was a crucial time. Not only was there a possibility of settling the New Guinea question in Matthew's favor, but the future of Oxford was to be determined.

At this point it would be instructive to take a more detailed look at Matthew's motivation for entering solitude, now that the whole question was being raised again. His motives were many and complex, as the following analysis indicates.

III.
The Road to Solitude

What would lead a gregarious, outgoing person like Matthew Kelty to a hermitage? The answers are found in a series of chapter and retreat talks given while he was a monk at Gethsemani. Some of these were duplicated for others to read, some never progressed beyond rough manuscripts. Written between 1967 and 1970, they reveal the steady development and evolution of his thinking on solitude.

It might be best to begin with an examination of Matthew's philosophy on the purpose of the monastic life. In a talk on "The Psalms as Prayer," given at Gethsemani in April, 1967, he said, "the monastery exists for one purpose: the contemplative experience. All of the elements in the monastic life such as prayer, manual labor, fasting, poverty, and the others, exist to accomplish one goal: the experience of God." Matthew realized that such an experience could never be legislated, but the monastery could provide the context wherein such an experience might take place.

People who visit monasteries are often impressed by the externals of the life: the architecture, the music, the habits, the obvious hard work that goes on. In this particular talk, however, Matthew made it clear that the most important features of monastic living exist within the monk himself. The Psalms, Matthew said, are difficult for many people because they expose the darkness within man. While many Christians are inspired by the lofty psalms of praise, the simplicity of the Twenty-Third Psalm, the moving, inward examination of psalms such as Psalm 139 ("O Lord, thou hast searched me and known me."), they know that the psalms also reflect "darkness, wrath, anger, hatred and vengeance, and a host of other unhappy qualities." (For examples, see Psalms 109 and 137.) But, these qualities are found in the hearts of people and we must face up to them.

"How are you going to cope with the forces recognized in your own depths? Forces of darkness? What are you going to do when it dawns on you that the words of David are true not only of David but of you? And having met these monsters, what if you cannot master them? The psalms are indeed strong meat, manly fare," Matthew told his Gethsemani brothers.

In the monastery, he believed, the monk experiences humanity "all the way in, all the way down." But most people do not know themselves this deeply and do not want to know. "They much prefer to live on a fragile surface with a workable bundle of adjustments they pass off to themselves and others as who they are." The psalms, however, "bring us face to face with the traitor in our own heart: the two-timer, the time server, the false friend. Who has not met the demon of envy, of jealousy, of greed, of hatred, lurking in the dark shadows of his depths, a side of himself that rarely comes into the light? And what appropriate words we find in the psalms to deal with these elements of Hell within us!"

The monk, Matthew felt, goes out into the desert,

which is the monastery, to confront these dark forces within his own depths. "A monk is called to reality and to the brave look at reality which is given the dignified name of contemplation."

For Matthew, the real justification of the monastic life was that "it is only by an experience of man as he truly is that we begin to know the beauty that surrounds him like a light of glory which is the love of God. It is only when you go into the wilderness with Jesus that life begins, and with that an awareness that without Him we are lost." And, Matthew knew, one only experiences these mysteries in solitude and seclusion.

Near the end of this talk Matthew predicted a renewal of interest in the contemplative life. "God Himself has sent a little chaos into the world and made of it in more ways than one a great wilderness. That being so, you may be sure that many will lose their faith, but, we will also see a growing interest in the contemplative life. But the interest will be in the contemplative experience, not just the plant and the setting, the words and the wherewithal."

Seven months later, on the occasion of the 101st anniversary of the dedication of the abbey church Matthew talked to his brothers about a Bob Dylan song, "Desolation Row." The song was about failure in love, and Matthew felt that we all live on Desolation Row, we have all failed in love. Yet, "it is by being wretched that we win the mercy of Christ and by admitting and accepting it that we are healed."

Modern people, he believed, were going to great lengths to escape from what they felt was the phoniness of life. Men entered monasteries, however, not to escape phoneyness, but to discover it. "When men in a monastery begin to discover the dimensions of their own running does not always seem to be the appropriate answer," he wrote. "Sooner or later you may have to stop running." In fact, he said, "in the moment of our defeat lies our triumph, in our ignominy lies our glory. And there in the midst of the shambles and ruin that is you, the Spirit of God will hover and turn all into a splendid vision."

Matthew applied the "Desolation Row" image to the monastic choir. In the Gethsemani church the monks stood in two rows on either side of the church, facing each other across the empty center. Here they chanted the psalms antiphonally as monks have done for centuries. The monks in white cowls, however, are human beings, merely men, with all the frailties of the flesh. As they look at each other across the empty center and sing psalms to each other they are confronted, face to face, with the realities of humanity, and the choir becomes another "Desolation Row." "We look across the avenue of the residents of Desolation Row and they look across at us. This is the inner city. This is the dialogue that matters. This is the desert waste, the asphalt jungle and the concrete nightmare. This is Appalachia and Detroit. In this wilderness we take our stand. It is no wonder that men have found this challenge awesome. This is no elfin song and dance routine. What a marvel that it should have perdured."

Matthew advised his brothers, "Why not listen a little? Why not slow down some, hush up a bit, sit still a moment, turn on your dreams and listen to the wind, to the woods, to the water? Bend over and look down into the dark pool of your own depths and do not be afraid. That is the purpose of a monastery."

What would this listening produce? It would produce an awareness of what we really are. "I suggested that as many as possible as soon as possible plunge into the desolation of their own hearts and learn what it is to be a Christian, to be a sinner in need of redemption rather than a pious man in need of praise. There is no joy akin to the joy of knowing the love of Christ. But this joy is impossible unless you know what street He lives on, Desolation Row."

On Christmas Eve, 1967, Matthew spoke to the monks about the forthcoming retirement of his first abbot. This man had served since the late 1940's and was now stepping down to take up the life of a hermit in the woods near Gethsemani. This would be the last Christmas the monks would spend with him as their spiritual leader. Matthew continued the theme that the monastery enables men to see things as they really are. "Lacking the pleasant distractions and diversions of the good life, we have more attention available for things that matter." This can be painful, for the monk will discover "that the dimensions of God's activity include much that is unfathomable." But for this the monk can give thanks for having come to know God better.

Monks discover more about the reality of God and more about the reality of man. "The whole of life seems to add up to a bundle of contradictions. This seems particularly true today when a strange Providence has decreed for our own time an element of chaos and confusion that at times seems to overwhelm us." However, discovering the terrible realities within man can bring peace to the individual, Matthew said, "because we discover that in the midst of reality sits the humble Savior, there in the bombed-out ruins of our own particular desolation, there in midst of the chaos and confusion of our time stands the humble Christ, serene, calm. His message is one of peace. It sounds almost out of place. Irreverent.

And yet I see Him and I hear Him say it."

This is why, Matthew believed, the abbot wanted to become a hermit. He wanted to be by himself, "not to nurse his wounds, not to count his victories, but rather quietly to take all the mysterious fabric of one's life and there lay it all out and trace the hand of love that somehow ordered all things, the good and the bad, the crooked and the straight, the bitter and the sweet, the whole of it . . . and then to take the whole thing and throw it over one as a garment woven in love."

So, we have an early mention of the hermit life and what its purpose might be. This interest would evolve and grow and be challenged and modified and finally flower.

In 1968 Matthew was sent to a sister monastery to lead a retreat. In his first talk, "The Poor Monk", he told the retreatants, "the monastic life has but one purpose and that is to discover reality." And how does the monk do this? He must remove from his vision "what is false and fraudulent, the artificial and constructed." But this is very hard to do, and many would rather not face reality. Reality can be frightening.

One of the themes that appeared frequently in Matthew's writings and letters was the harshness of God. It would seem, he often said, that God makes the existence of some people very miserable. He told of a brother in his monastery who lived a good monastic life and was faithful to his vows. He was given a job he did not know much about, but he worked hard at it and gradually became more skillful. One day the monks were all given chest X-rays. When the reports came back it was discovered that this faithful brother had a hopeless case of lung cancer.

Matthew told the retreatants of friends he knew in

Boston who had worked their way out of poverty during the Depression. "I never knew such a poor family. They were poor poor." Finally, they prospered and had two children. The boy went to Viet Nam and was killed. Later the father was in an accident and lost a leg. Misery came upon misery for these good, hard working people. "It is a hard world for many," Matthew said. "It is a world full of mystery and darkness. The Lord made the night too long for a lot of people."

He mentioned a common family problem during the 1960's. Parents work hard for their children. Finally they succeed, only to find out that their children do not want material things. The world's goods have no appeal, and the children live by a set of values the parents cannot begin to understand. "The monk got this message early. His style was a bit neater and he did not have to go through all the antics of hair and beads. But he got the word and got it soon, that what the world offers is not much. There must be something better."

This is what the monastic life is all about. It was for Matthew, a way "to meet the will of God head-on and direct, not by standing around waiting for it to happen to you, but by anticipating it, by walking right into it. That is indeed to master life and to come to know its secret."

So the monk went into the desert where there was freedom. He looked around and there was only himself and God. And then began what Matthew called "earth's loveliest dialogue" between the individual and God, "the sweet exchange of intimacies between pauper and the prince. Of this, every human love affair is but a faint echo, a small version, a sample and test run."

The greatest obstacle man faces in his desire for God is fear. "We are literally frightened to death. We fear God, man, ourselves, time, eternity, life and death." And with this fear the monk sees new meaning in the beatitude, "Blessed are the poor in spirit."

The monk, however, faces this fear; he walks right into the middle of it. To his retreatants Matthew said, "You have gone into the depths of one's own heart and have come to know what is there: the region of darkness, the deep where the monsters dwell, the hell into which Christ descended after the death on the cross before He rose on the third day. For you must not only die with Him, but you must descend into the depths with Him if you are to rise. This is what the monk does."

What makes one a monk is "the ability to grasp total reality." It is the poverty and wretchedness within man that makes the love of God so wonderful. In finding that love the monk becomes aware of God in new and dynamic ways. Matthew concluded this talk by saying, "The presence of God is all around us, in us, among us, in the hills and in the woods, in the blight and in the burden, in the sorrow and in the laughter. We can laugh then, with Christ, and shed tears with him. Walk on the waters, and go up to Tabor, in the garden of olives and at Cana. With him all the way. All the time. Poor. And ours is the Kingdom."

One of the finest pieces Matthew wrote was a talk on the monastic life called "There Must be an Element of Madness in our Life." What did he mean by madness? Certainly he did not mean that all is madness and therefore nothing really matters. "On the contrary it means a great sober seriousness, a serious approach to prayer, to choir, to work, to reading, to silence, and to everything else that is part of life." In the monastic sense madness was a "refusal to submit everything to cold reason as the ultimate norm." The saints, he pointed out, all realized that there comes a time when reason is useless and man must move beyond it.

By the normal standards of American society monks are mad and a monastery is a madhouse. What do monks do that is so mad? Matthew gave a long list. "They get up at 2:00 in the morning. They spend hours every day singing songs to God. They sing them in an ancient and forgotten melody. They are celibate, virginal, they never marry, have no wives, no children. They do not talk as other men talk. They do not eat as other men eat. They drink no beer, watch no TV, play no games, never sit around and chat. They live in peace with their brothers, do not fight, do not strike back, bear correction, suffer wrong, endure insult, turn the other cheek." Madness, indeed.

Why do the monks do these things? "They are in love," Matthew answered. "They do mad things because people who are in love do mad things. There is no other way that love can speak. This is the language of love. It is not necessary. It is not reasonable. It is not in accord with common sense. All very true. It is simply the way of men who are in love. That is all."

He then explained why he changed from a reasonable life to a life of madness. "When I led a reasonable life in which everything made sense it followed by the very nature of things that the God I knew and loved and served was also reasonable. He was good and kind and tender and merciful and most of all, reasonable."

But then, as a priest and a missionary Matthew began to work among "the common people of the world," which were, of course, everyone. Here he encountered "death and disease and anguish of every kind: men with no work, families whose fathers simply walked out on them, wives who lost their minds, mothers whose little children were taken in death, men and women putting up with dreadful conditions in their families, their homes, their neighborhood, their work, their parishes, and having to put up with them, simply having to live with them. All these good people, not wretched sinners living in vice and debauchery, but good, good people."

In this context God no longer seemed reasonable; he became even more mysterious. Talk of a reasonable God was no comfort or help, for all that Matthew saw around him was irrational. So he moved to a madhouse, a monastery.

"I thought this place was mad and full of men loving a God who was also mad," he wrote. "And then I suddenly realized the meaning of it all. When your life in grace is governed by reason and the reasonable beyond a certain point you lose your touch with God. You are out of context with Him. You no longer speak His language. When He speaks you do not hear Him. When He acts you do not comprehend. You miss entirely the workings of God because you are in the fog of earthly life. But when you operate in the area of madness you begin to speak a language that God speaks."

To find God we must move beyond reason, for the ways of God are not our ways. He does things in his own way. But that really does not matter. The one thing we need to know is that God loves us. The monastic life, for Matthew, was not an end in itself. It simply made it possible "to embrace the action of God which to human understanding is often sheer madness." But, in all the madness "we must find God somehow, or else we are doomed to a dull, meaningless life."

Matthew concluded this talk by asking his brothers when the last time something unreasonable happened to them. When were they last abused or treated unfairly or dealt with unjustly? Then he said, "I might just as well ask: when last did God kiss you? Embrace you? For this is the kind of thing that happens every day to the thousands of people we call the faithful. They see the hand of God in all this because they have to. We do not have to. We are invited to. If we do not, we miss the whole point. We do not know God and do not understand how He operates. Do not know when He has His arms around us."

"If we cannot recognize God in the madness of life we have much to learn. And the monastery is a good school. The madness that we know in the way we live is simply to get us in shape and keep us in trim for the most magnificent work a man can do: come in contact with God."

"We do not have to understand Him, but a little madness in our life will be a great help, will lead us into the depths of the great good Lord, the loving God of mystery, of the Infinite, the child in the crib who will come to judge us all. And in this too we will keep the common touch that makes us one with our neighbors in kissing the holy hands that lay a cross upon our back."

For all of its glories, the monastic life also has its hazards. "There are many false solutions and blind alleys. Failures abound." The monk, in order to survive, must recognize that that life is a "complete gift which consists in always living to the ultimate." By this Matthew did not mean just an unusual zeal and ardor in daily living. Rather he spoke of "an inner meeting of all forces at a kind of fusing point which must be held with all one's resources at just that juncture where the flame of God's loving presence burns with glorious intensity. It is that or nothing at all."

As early as 1967 Matthew was already thinking a good

bit about the hermit life. On October 17 he expressed doubts about small group monastic living, but was aware that there was a strong trend toward this style of monasticism developing. Oxford, of course, would be one manifestation of that movement. But in 1967 he saw it as a passing fad.

One reason for this judgement was Matthew's awareness that the desire for smaller communities was an expression of a search for the heart. The hope was that free from the distractions of a large community the monk might see more deeply into his own heart. But Matthew felt that once this began to happen the monk would find even the small group "intolerable and stifling." The next step would be a desire for the hermit life with "its concern for meeting all of the forces of heaven and hell, time and eternity, in the soul."

He predicted a flowering of the hermit life. "Since the eremetical life is the logical follow-up of the communal life, we can prepare to see a great flourishing of hermits, men committed to an entirely solitary life, engaged in the dialogue of love not through any fears or by way of flight but by an ability to hold their ground alone by dint of the experience of love in the community. After all, the hermit life is simply a continuation of response to the original call to leave all and follow Christ." After long training and formation in the monastery where the monk experienced love among his brothers, the hermit would move into solitude "to resolve the hidden ambiguities and conflicts in a bold and naked contact with pure love, frail man naked before God Almighty." The toleration and support of the hermit by the monastic community was a test, Matthew believed, of the monastery's authenticity. "Hermits are the glory of the monastery and the evidence that the place is real."

Without indicating any personal calling to it, Matthew spoke more specifically about the hermit life in a talk he gave on the Dalai Lama and a book he had read about Tibet. He explained the progress a monk might make in his spiritual growth. If the monk continues to develop he might grow out of the common life. Some monks misunderstood what was happening to them and left the monastery. Others were drawn to the hermitage. A monk who did this, said Matthew, was "in some way acting out what was going on within him, and put into action what was being acted out in his own heart."

He warned his brothers that the call to solitude might come to them and they might not understand it. "Slowly and strangely something will come over you and you will be frightened by it." But, he said, "This is necessary and wholly a healthy development in our spiritual life and one we must learn to recognize and appreciate. It is an invitation by divine grace to move further in and deeper down. It is a call to further abandonment and deeper commitment."

He told the monks, however, that any call to solitude had to be confirmed by "God's agents," that is, their ecclesiastical or monastic superiors. Matthew affirmed this in his own experience. He refused to go to New Guinea until an abbot said yes. In the long run, however, it appeared that things had worked out for the best and the slow route to solitude was the right one.

The solitary life, he agreed, was not for everyone. Certainly the call to the hermitage did not make the solitary superior to anyone else. It was simply a different style.

Matthew often used the image of dance. "What happens is that while you dance the whole thing has changed. It is not only that you feel yourself disappearing, but your partner disappears, the people in the ballroom disappear, the roof goes off the place, and the whole thing opens up to infinite dimensions so that you feel truly as if you were dancing in heaven itself. And yet you dance still. The divine aspect of the life on earth becomes manifest and obvious. But this vision is never possible without a genuine death, without a farewell to everything you have loved, without a giving away of all that is dear to you."

When he finally decided that he wanted the hermitage, why did Matthew choose New Guinea? There were several obvious reasons. He knew the area, the bishop was his friend, there would be a sense of exile. But there was another reason, and it began to surface in chapter talks and later in his letters. He believed that primitive man was more in touch with spiritual reality because he was free of the distractions of civilization.

In one of his talks called "The Monastic Choir as Song and Dance," he compared the ritual of the monastic Divine Offices and the processions of the monks with the ceremonial dances of primitives. Dancing, he said, put one into the rhythm of the universe. Primitive man "has caught the rhythm of life, and though he has caught but a part of it, he has caught a great deal. In fact, many Christians who know a great deal about a great many things often do not have the appreciation of the fundamentals that many a primitive has."

"When the monks seek God," Matthew said, "they will find him. And when they find Him you need not worry about them singing or dancing. They will sing and dance until they drop. Only to carry on in the Kingdom of Heaven."

During the Easter season in 1968 Matthew spoke to his community on "Liturgy and the Fatherless Generation." In less than a year he would raise the question of his own move into solitude. While this talk dealt with other matters, specifically liturgy as love making with God, he mentioned very briefly his own feelings about the hermit life. He described the monastery as a "school for love" where the monk might prepare for "the still more noble life of solitude in the hermit cell." Not all monks would agree, of course, that the solitary life was any more noble, but Matthew felt that in it "one engages directly in dialogue with the love of God." Anticipating his own forthcoming request he repeated what he had said in earlier talks, that "the test of the monastery's authenticity will lie in its response to the call to solitude." An authentic community would not hold back one whom God has called to the hermitage.

He was aware, however, of the dangers. In a homily on the resurrection he warned that "It is in being quiet, in being alone, in being apart that we discover that we have no faith and no hope and no love. No wonder then that men sometimes fear solitude and silence and seclusion." But the picture is not all that bad. To know that we have no faith is to beg for it, to feel that we have no grace will lead us to petition. To learn that we have no love is to realize the need for a Redeemer. To find out that was to come a long way indeed, and was the first giant step to a living faith.

One of the recurring themes in Matthew's writing was the inward discovery of the human condition. The monk could not make any serious progress until he could honestly face up to the real nature of man and see both the good and evil that reside deep within the human spirit. In a talk on "The Monastic Technique" he noted that "this can come only by contact with our deepest side. The side that most quickly comes into view in the hours of silence and loneliness, in the quiet of the night, the peace of a natural surrounding. This we must welcome, must love, must embrace. It is the key to freedom."

Early in 1969 Matthew entered into discussions with his abbot and his friends about whether he should go to New Guinea to live as a hermit. In October of that year he duplicated a statement to send to friends titled "Genesis of a Solitary Vocation: A Personal Journey." In it he summarized both his reasons and the abbey's objections, appealing to his brother monks for their support and confidence in his quest for solitude.

He began by explaining his growth in the desire for the solitary life and his conviction that it was the will of God. He reported his decision to wait until he had been at Gethsemani for ten years before attempting to make a move. His abbot, he said, was willing to let him go, but was not enthusiastic. For the moment, the decision was Matthew's.

The bulk of the document contained Matthew's answers to the objections raised against him.

1. He was not attempting to return to the SVD, his missionary order, nor did he want to go back to apostolic life.

2. He was not disenchanted with Gethsemani. There was no sense of failure about his monastic vocation. In fact, Matthew said, "I see the call to solitude as a further expression and refinement of that monastic calling."

3. He did not believe himself to have any individual merit that made him superior to those who live in monasteries. He presented his own self-evaluation. "As an SVD priest and missionary, as also a monk, I have hardly been more than average or below average. As a hermit or solitary also, I do not expect I will do much better. But I do not think that should cause concern. God can work through anyone."

4. One of the strongest reasons given for staying at Gethsemani was that the monastery needed his talents. However, he insisted that there was no better way for him to help the abbey but to do the will of God. "Am I to suppose that the God who brought me here in the first place is not able to take my place? I think we must have a little faith and a little generosity and courage. For all that, is it to be assumed that only they can become solitaries whom the community cannot use? I am not saying that I am a spellbinder and a great jewel in Gethsemani's crown. I am saying only that if a monk does his part and can pull his oar, it ought not to be held against him."

5. In no way should his desire to leave be interpreted as hostility toward the abbey. "I am not disillusioned or disappointed. People who say I do not like the life do not know me. People who say I never liked the place are not with the truth." He simply hoped that the abbey would be "a mother whose love for her sons is not grasping and strangling."

6. Is this really the will of God? "I do not know," answered Matthew. "But I believe it is. I have done all I could. I have spent this year in intensive prayer and study of the question. I have discussed, written, done my best to keep open. In the end what can you do? You can only take the chance and the risk. But I am convinced that the hand of the Lord is in this."

7. It should be no problem for someone else to take over the editorship of *Monastic Exchange*.

8. Matthew was often accused of being an erratic person. His answer: "Some say I am erratic. Well, it is quite possible. In that case, going or staying would not make any difference."

9. Was this longing for solitude just a romantic fantasy? Matthew acknowledged that it might be. "There is no question that the romantic aspects of the solitary life appeal to me. A little hermitage by the sea. Or in the mountains. A brook. A wood. My little chapel. My icon, or image. My fire. A few books. My flute. And my solitude and silence and seclusion. It is all very lovely. Idyllic. Would turn anybody on. And in a tropic setting even more so. Thatched roof hut, swaying palms."

People who knew him for the social, talkative, articulate person that he was had serious doubts that he could survive in solitude. That was an important consideration. Matthew explained that his social side had become fully developed. However, people did not realize that there was another side to his personality which he now wanted to develop. He admitted that when he faced solitude in New Guinea during his missionary days he was too immature to handle it. But now he was ready. As long as he lived in community with other people his solitary aspect would never grow. So, he must now go into hiding. He hoped to do so with the support of his brothers and his abbot. Without it he doubted that he would survive.

Matthew had worked it all out in his mind. He had explored the question thoroughly for a year, satisfied himself that he was doing the will of God. But, it was not to be, at least for the present. Lacking what he thought was adequate support, although no one ever told him absolutely that he could not become a hermit, he decided to remain at Gethsemani. The hermitage was a nice dream, but apparently it was not realistic. Monastic obedience sometimes exacted a high price.

Looking back over these events Matthew would later see that God works in ways not always obvious at the moment. The Oxford experience proved to be a valuable transition between large abbey and hermitage. "I think all worked out in the providence of God," he wrote to me in a personal letter from New Guinea. "The abbot did OK by me. The Oxford experience was superb and perfect toward coming here."

In 1969, of course, Matthew could not see into the future. He did not know that Oxford lay ahead or that in less than five years he would actually be in New Guinea.

IV.
New Guinea Hermitage

"O God . . . look upon this thy son and bless thy servant, Matthew, who by this silver ring hath taken to himself Holy Solitude as Bride and Companion of his heart, to have and to hold from this day forward . . . . Grant that he may always be faithful to her and she to him, so that in his love for her he may find thee alone."

With this prayer there concluded an unusual marriage ceremony, in a monastery of all places. But this was not a wedding of man and woman; it was a marriage of a man and solitude. Matthew Kelty pledged his troth to Holy Solitude, a mysterious, demanding, yet silent bride. The day was June 23, 1973, and the next day, the feast of John the Baptist, another solitary, he said farewell to his brothers at Gethsemani. The longed for and elusive day had come at last. But we are ahead of our story.

After three years at Oxford Matthew had become very fond of the little monastery. It is true that no one would stay with him on a permanent basis, but many people moved in and out of the community. Monks, priests, SVD novices, college students, and other guests appeared with great regularity, bringing diversity and freshness to the monastery. The reputation of the place was growing.

Occasional articles in the Raleigh *News and Observer* and the Durham *Herald* gradually made people aware of Matthew's presence. He was never overwhelmed with visitors, but some regular guests began to make periodic retreats. A genuine appreciation for the place began to develop in eastern North Carolina on the part of many people, most of whom were not Catholics, some of whom were not even Christians.

When the word arrived that the abbot of Gethsemani would retire a sense of uncertainty began to settle over Oxford. What would the future bring? There had never been great enthusiasm at Gethsemani for the Oxford experiment and Matthew knew it. He described the little monastery as a "frail craft" that might sink or be swamped at any moment.

Matthew still harbored a desire to go to New Guinea. True, he was alone at Oxford most of the time now, but, small as it was, it was too much for one man to maintain. Still, if New Guinea was out of the question, Oxford was probably the next best thing. So, it was with surprise and renewed hope that in March, 1973, Matthew received a letter from the newly elected abbot, just two weeks in office, offering to reopen the question of Matthew's future. The abbot even indicated that he would consider the idea of exile, but such a decision should not be made quickly.

Containing enthusiasm was not one of Matthew's strong skills, but he attempted to respond calmly. He knew that his prayers had now been answered and that he would go to New Guinea. Still, nothing was settled yet. The whole project would have to be discussed by the Abbot's Council.

In any event, the new abbot promised to visit Oxford, look over the facilities, and talk with Matthew about his future. At the same time another monk was planning to move from Gethsemani to Oxford. Matthew's leaving might make this brother's stay relatively brief.

The abbot asked Matthew to write and describe his present feelings about his vocation, saying that nothing would be said to the Gethsemani community for a few weeks. Matthew responded by repeating the same story of his developing interest in solitude, his decision to wait until he had been at Gethsemani for ten years before making any formal request, and his desire for exile. The former abbot had left the decision up to Matthew, but would not personally endorse it. Matthew admitted that he was disappointed, and when Oxford came up he was rather luke-warm about it, having no particular interest in small community monastic living. Now, however, he could see that it was of great value. The loneliness of Oxford enabled him to think things over more calmly and pray more deeply. And he was still convinced that the hermitage was the will of God for him.

Matthew, of course, was ready to go immediately. He even hoped that he could leave on June 24, the anniversary of his vows at Gethsemani, but that was not to be. There were many preparations ahead. Immigration procedures, the disposal of Oxford, and a firm agreement between Archbishop Noser and Gethsemani all had to be worked out. He even had an idea that he would ride his Honda across the country, visiting monasteries along the way as sort of a last farewell and then sail from the West Coast to New Guinea. But that was not to be either.

Among the many friends Matthew had made was a young married couple, recently graduated from the University of Notre Dame. This couple, very devoted Catholics, developed plans to move to New Guinea as lay teachers in a mission school for a three to five year term.

After their arrival in New Guinea in the Spring of 1973

they wrote to Matthew, asking about the abbatial election at Gethsemani and wondering what the new man's attitude might be toward the hermit life. "Might we see you here in New Guinea?" they asked. Later the couple wrote and described their work and living conditions. They noted that their school was near the village of Malala, eighty miles north of Madang. There was no road from there to Madang, but there was one to a place called Bogia. Little did they know at the time that Matthew would settle there.

On April 6 Matthew wrote to Archbishop Noser to ask if the invitation previously extended was still open. The Archbishop replied affirmatively. He told Matthew that for visa purposes he should come as a missionary. Once there, he could make his own selection of a hermitage site. The Archbishop wanted Matthew free to choose his own situation, only suggesting that he pick a spot where obtaining supplies would not be a problem.

Archbishop Noser expressed again to Matthew his concern that the Christians of New Guinea understand the importance of prayer and self-sacrifice in the Christian life. Even these people, living in an underdeveloped nation, had become very materialistic. It was essential that there be a contemplative witness. Preaching was not enough; prayer and self-denial must undergird it.

Meanwhile, the abbot of Gethsemani was planning a visit to Oxford in late May. Now he could talk with Matthew face to face about his vocation and at the same time look into the question of the future of Oxford, about which Bishop Waters in Raleigh was very concerned.

Matthew was impatient. He was ready to go to New Guinea, but the decision making process in religious institutions moves slowly. Perhaps one of the lessons to be learned from Matthew's experience was patience. God does things at his own speed, and what seems like need-less delay often turns out to have a purpose. It can never be said that Matthew rushed into solitude without giving it adequate thought. He might have, but his commitment to obedience prevented it. He would not go until he had the solid blessing and backing of his community and superiors. He now began to sense that the abbot's position was "not red, not green; sort of amber: proceed with caution."

Some of the brothers at Gethsemani still worried about Matthew's restlessness. Others feared that he was headed for the active ministry. The new abbot insisted that Matthew should depend upon Gethsemani for his support and not a local bishop. For himself, Matthew had some anxiety about the future of Oxford, a place he had come to love deeply. During these weeks of uncertainty Matthew's abbot advised him to trust in the Holy Spirit to work the problems out.

On June 7, 1973, the abbot wrote to Matthew and told him the good news. The House Council at Gethsemani had discussed the matter for an hour and had decided unanimously that Matthew should be allowed to go to New Guinea to live as a solitary. The only real condition was that he maintain contact with the order either through periodic visits to another monastery or by being visited by someone in the order. It was also agreed that he would receive his support from Gethsemani and would not cultivate supporters in New Guinea. At the same time it was decided that the Oxford monastery would be turned over to the Cistercian North American Region with the hope that some other Trappist house might take it.

The years of hoping and waiting were over. What Matthew believed to be the will of God had come to pass. Patience had been rewarded. Looking back over the events of his life one can easily discern a pattern. The focus of his existence steadily narrowed: active missionary, editor, monk in large abbey, monk in small community, hermit. From that vantage point the journey to New Guinea appears to have been inevitable.

Now preparations for departure had to begin. First, Matthew wrote to Archbishop Noser and received a "Deo Gratias" response. The Archbishop offered some practical advice on applying for passport and visa. His friends, the lay couple, wrote offering their congratulations and welcome. Brothers from Gethsemani and the SVD responded warmly to the news. North Carolinians who visited Oxford were disappointed that he would be leaving, but wished him well and offered their prayers.

Archbishop Noser recommended that Matthew bring his mission trunk which he still had from his former days in New Guinea. Matthew should fill it with whatever books he might need as books were very expensive in the area. He should also bring his typewriter. It was suggested, however, that he take very little in way of clothing, buying what he needed after arrival.

In August, 1973 the Archbishop officially wrote to the abbot of Gethsemani explaining the arrangements. He made it clear that he did not want Matthew to engage in apostolic work, but to support the missionary effort by living to the fullest the life of a Trappist monk as a solitary. Matthew would be allowed to choose the site for his hermitage after he arrived. An existing structure could be remodeled, or a new one built. It would be simple but practical. The Archbishop also pledged that if Matthew found the hermit life impossible, he would be allowed to return to Gethsemani.

Meanwhile, Matthew, Bishop Waters, and Gethsemani began casting about for someone to take over Oxford. Many groups expressed interest in the idea, but found it impossible to actually move to a new place. For a while it looked like no one would move into the little monastery. Finally, after a number of refusals from other places a Trappist house in Massachusetts, St. Joseph's Abbey, agreed to look over the situation. The abbot made a visit, and a group of monks who already supported themselves by making vestments decided to come in the Fall. Oxford would continue.

In late June, 1973, Matthew returned to Gethsemani for a final visit, although it would be several months before he would actually leave for New Guinea. On June 23, before the abbot and the prior, Matthew went through the ceremony of marriage to Holy Solitude. Appropriately, he put on a silver wedding band. On the outside was inscribed "O Beata Solitudo," and on the inside "Matthew Kelty - Gethsemani." Whatever happened in the future, he wanted it clear that he was a monk of Gethsemani.

June had always been an important month in his life. On June 21, thirty-four years earlier, he had taken his first vows as a missionary to the SVD. On June 24, eleven years earlier, he had taken his solemn vows at Gethsemani. Three years ago on that date he had left Kentucky for Oxford. Now he was telling his brother monks good-bye on that date. Not to be forgotten, of course, was that June 24 was the feast day of John the Baptist, one who had lived in the desert as a solitary prior to announcing the ministry of Jesus.

On June 24, 1973, Matthew delivered a talk in chapter to the Gethsemani community in which he described his feelings about moving to New Guinea. Faith, he told his brothers, involves an element of risk. "There is no following Jesus without the step into darkness. You have to go down if you want to go up. If you want Him you have to give everything away. If you want to be robed in glory you have to strip. You have to be free and available. Hold out your hand, receive what you are given, give what you have. Wholly. Totally. It is great joy, great peace. Total love."

In that talk he expressed his love for Gethsemani. "My God, this is a beautiful place. I daresay yesterday had anyone come to me and told me I was nuts, that I should give up this dizzy business of going off alone someplace and settle down here and be a monk, I daresay I would have taken him up on it. I had a weak moment or two. I am a weak character. People like me need vows and rings and things."

He also offered opinions on Oxford. "I think the three years Gethsemani has been there have made a successful experiment. As far as I see it, it proves that Cistercian life can be lived fruitfully and richly in a minimum context of small land, few buildings, simple style, few monks. It means we are not frozen to the large holding, big plant, handsome liturgy." He spoke of the reaction of people in eastern North Carolina to Oxford. "Oxford is much loved by many people. It has a message. It is a vine God planted. It has some meaning. So pray that all works out happily."

He described his travel plans. "I go by ship. I insist. I am not zooming by jet into solitude." The decision about going had taken a long time. There was no reason to rush into anything now.

There was a personal note. His sister, to whom he was closest in the family, had taken the decision well. "I am glad for that. It is not pleasant when your kin weeps over you."

That morning Matthew had officiated at the community High Mass. It was the feast of Corpus Christi, and there was a procession through the cloister with the sacrament. It was quite fitting, he said. "We take a last walk together, and we take the Lord with us as we go. We begin the journey together. You walk a mile with me and see me off down the road."

He told the monks about the large cross that had been erected in the little meadow at Oxford. Christmas tree balls were suspended from each arm. "On Summer Solstice one of the balls fell gently to the ground. Well, Charlie, I said to myself, there you have it. When the fruit is ripe and ready it falls to the ground. Your time has come. This is the point of three years at Oxford. The fruit falls to become the seed of new life, of new beauty."

With those words Matthew departed Gethsemani, never expecting to see the monastery again. He returned to Oxford to bring things to a close and to prepare to sail.

The summer of 1973 was spent filing for passport and visa, trying to get the Oxford monastery in good shape for the arrival of new monks, and saying good-bye to friends.

On Holy Cross Day, September 14, 1973, Matthew sent out another newsletter, bringing his friends up to date on events. Describing the action of the abbot and his council Matthew reported, "They agreed with me that New Guinea offered the best situation in terms of exile, the hearty welcome of the archbishop, the climate, the lack of any monastic witness there, the fact that I had been a missionary there some twenty-five years ago."

He listed the things he planned to take with him. His flute, which he often played at Mass at Oxford, would go along. The bishop had suggested some books, so Matthew bought the Oxford set of the *Encyclopedia Britannica* and some volumes of Karl Jung. A nephew had given him a set of the Great Books that would increase his library. In addition, "some versions of Scripture I had, some commentaries, and a few other books filled a box. The box, incidentally, that I brought along from the SVD in 1960 when I joined the monastery. A mission chest made by the Brothers (SVD) in the shop at Techny, a beautiful piece of work: all the missionaries used to get one in the old days." He also hoped to do weaving there, but would have to see how the situation developed. Taking a big loom was out of the question.

A week before the letter was written Matthew had returned from a visit with his family in Boston. "The family keeps growing all the time," he wrote, "and I am much out of touch. Many I have not seen in years. It is something of a shock to see someone after an interval of ten or twenty or even longer terms of years. I guess the most amazing thing is to discover traits of character or disposition or physical qualities passed on from one generation to the next. With skips and leaps, of course, and odd combinations and mixtures. Life goes on. A beautiful mystery."

He enjoyed the trip, but was happy to return to Oxford. "I was away only a week and glad to be back. I am much attached to the pace of the life here in the woods and relish the quiet. The Harvest Moon was in glory and this place at night, as I came into it, was really a spectacle. Looked hauntingly beautiful, had a gentle mysterious touch." Oxford had grown on Matthew Kelty.

As he prepared to leave for New Guinea he wrote, "I feel a great peace. I am not specially excited. Not nearly so much as the first time out to New Guinea twenty-five years ago. Yet, I have the feeling that everything is as it should be. As if it were all planned. In a way my life gets smaller: from the active missionary order to the contemplative abbey. From the large abbey to this little monastery in the woods. From here to solitude in New Guinea. But I guess it is an expanding life too, in that I sense an identity with the whole Church and the whole human family. I simply experience a sort of unity — I do not feel alone or alienated or apart."

The last letter to be written from Oxford by Matthew appeared in the Fall, 1973 issue of *Monastic Exchange*. He described the new monks who would soon arrive and the visit their abbot had made. "All this," he wrote, "is, of course, a happy development and one that will please a great many people. The monastery will be ten years old this coming year and though its history has been somewhat unsteady, there has been a continuing monastic life here all the time. Perhaps a certain note of fragility is part of the small place. It tends to force one into a trust in Providence and a waiting on the Lord's good will."

He noted what visitors and monks alike had found out, that life at Oxford was hard. "It is difficult in this environment to escape the needs of the community or the demands of solitude. One must work in both areas and the whole tends to develop an awareness of reality that is fundamental to spiritual growth. When both the inner and outer man are alive in a healthy way, movement toward finding God in all things is rapid. There is no doubt in my mind that while this growth is possible anywhere, and most certainly in a good monastery, there is a certain intensity to the whole thing in a small place. It gives a quality to the life that is most enriching, if demanding.

Matthew announced that he expected to sail from New York on November 6, arriving in Sydney, Australia on November 25. He would visit monks there and then take a ship to New Guinea, hopefully settling into his house by Christmas. He was told by Archbishop Noser that many of the natives had left the bush and moved to the cities for economic reasons. Consequently, there were a number of abandonded mission stations back in the hills with no people around, any of which would serve as a good hermitage.

He admitted that "breaking loose of this place has been somewhat difficult. I have grown to love it very much. It is truly a lovely spot." The stress and frustration of attempting the New Guinea move over the years were now forgotten. "All things have their time. I have a great peace and feel that things are moving along the way they should be, in accord with God's designs. God will not be hurried and one must learn to wait on Him. The Summer was rather difficult in many ways, what with everything up in the air. But when things did begin to shape up, they did so very fast. Almost too fast."

The closing word to his friends was, "My love to you. The world is very small. A little love embraces the whole of it. And so we can touch one another in God. New Guinea is an emerging nation, a little one. The church is flourishing, but there is not yet a monastic witness. Please God there soon will be. Pray that it will be a valid one."

He took his leave of Oxford on the first of October, 1973. A few days were spent camping on the Outer Banks of North Carolina, walking the lonely beach. From there he rode to Plymouth, Massachusetts, and had a nice long visit with his sister. Then he spent some time alone on Cape Cod and in Maine, trying to prepare himself for a momentous change in his life. A trip West was aborted by bad weather, so the Honda was left with a priest friend who sold it for him.

Papua New Guinea was one of two remaining United Nations trust territories in 1973, administered by Australia. About a year after Matthew's arrival it would achieve independence and self-government. Comprising an area of 178,260 square miles, it has a population of about 2.6 million. There are approximately 1,000 different tribes divided into hundreds of language groups. A Trappist mission there was attempted in 1904-05, but was aborted when one of the brothers was killed in an uprising of natives. The other Trappist there was recalled to Bosnia.

On November 19 Matthew Kelty sailed from New York aboard the *Austral Envoy*, a container-cargo freighter and arrived in Australia in the middle of December. There were only twelve passengers on the ship, mostly retired people.

Only one stop was made, at Panama. The voyage took twenty-two days. "Ship life was quiet and restrained, the officers and crew friendly enough."

An airplane flight brought him to New Guinea on Christmas Eve, twenty-five years after his first trip there as a missionary. So much had happened in those intervening years, things that he could not possibly have foreseen.

The rest of this story can best be told by Matthew himself. His own letters make up the final chapter of this book. We can read in his own words an account of his solitary life.

V.
Letters From a Hermit

I received the following letters from Matthew over a period of almost four years. They tell, in his own words, the story of his move from the Oxford monastery to his New Guinea hermitage. For the most part, personal references have been deleted, but otherwise they are exactly as he wrote them.

1.

June 15, 1973

Dear Bill:

Just a note to say that I have just gotten word from my abbot that I may go solo to New Guinea! His council agreed unanimously! Had an hour's good discussion on it, abbot said. All went nicely.

Gethsemani is terminating the experiment here and turning it over to the monasteries of the Region if they like, or to other monastic group. I am confident it will continue. This and the above are both good matters to include in your prayers.

I went to D.C. and filed for passport. By bike. Good trip. Rides well.

Expect late summer departure, will be here to see new group in.

I feel at peace. As far as I am concerned, the experiment has been a success. It seems to make evident that Cistercian life can be lived on small piece of land, in a few simple buildings, with few monks, in simple style. And that such a style is both rewarding and demanding. This sets us free from any notion that we must be big if we are to survive. Should troubled days be coming, it is good to know we could carry on, simply traveling light. I like big houses; they last longer, stand up better. And history is on their side. But the little place has a lot going for it and a few years may see more of them.

The place is history now; the model exists. Its day will come. I do not think it my work. Father Peter planted a very good garden. I simply cultivated it three years, making only a few adjustments. But it has been a wonderful experience and I have joy in it.

Love to you all,
Matthew

2.

This letter was written after my family and I had made a final, farewell visit to Oxford. The article mentioned was one I wrote about him that later appeared in a college literary journal.

August 7, 1973

Dear Friends:

Nice visit. Thanks a lot. Looked like a row of daffodils or better, buttercups, standing in a line when I came out.

I liked the article. Rings well. Never thought of that before, that my circle narrows as it deepens. From mission work to monastery to this little place to solitude. Good route.

I dicker seriously with the thought of taking a loom along. I like the idea of having some craft I can pay my own way with. I am going up to Techny (the SVD house near Chicago) and I am going to mention it. They will know something of that project in New Guinea involving weaving. I had simply thought it unreal to consider carrying on with weaving out there; now I have second thoughts.

I am very happy for my contact with you, with the school, your town. It will abide. Carry it with me. It is a small world. Not hard to put your arms around it. Same sun that shines here, shines there. Same moon. We turn just as fast around the axis down there as here. It will be good to think of you and remember you in God's grace, that other world of love we live in which has quite another dimension than the one we occupy in space. I guess

that world is rather more real. And perduring.
My love to you all. Thanks for coming by.

In the Lord,
Matthew

3.

September 13, 1973

Dear B.P.:
A wretched way to answer a letter, but I want to tell you that three or four New England monks arrive next week to carry on. They are vestment makers and will move into weaving. Good! No priest, so they'll go to Mass in Oxford and communicate daily. Maybe later a priest will come. I sail out of New York on November 6 by freighter. Should be in New Guinea by Christmas. God is good. Things work out in time. My love to all and my thanks.

Matthew

4.

This is a letter I received from Matthew after his arrival in New Guinea. He had been there about two and a half months.

March 3, 1974

Dear Bill:

I am ashamed to think it is already March and it has been so long since I wrote you. For all that, it seems such a long time since last October when I left Oxford. I had planned a trip across country or at least to several of the monasteries and kith and kin, but that fell through. For one thing there was a delay with my passport and visa and I had the awful feeling that they might not come through, in which case leave-taking would have been ludicrous! And when I did finally set out I ran into cold and winds and snow and turned back. Too late for motorcycle. But I did have a long time with my sole sister in Plymouth, Massachusetts, some time on Cape Cod and down Maine. Very good.

I sailed out of New York on November 19, had a pleasant trip across the Pacific and landed in Melbourne on December 15. We stopped at New Zealand, and I visited the monks there as well as those in Australia: sheep farmers, simple, non-mystical types. Beautiful quiet places both. Hearty, down-to-earth, outdoor people. Landed here in Papua New Guinea on Christmas Eve, spent a month at headquarters in Alexishaven, then up here to Bogia.

I am to settle on a hilltop back of the coconut plantation on the site of the mission before the war. It was all destroyed and afterward they opted for the shore: a lovely view of the coast, islands, a volcano twelve miles off shore. Good breeze, rather remote and yet close to all I need. Mission station here below is fully equipped with big plantation, house, convent, school (300 pupils), teachers' houses, store — plus the plantation, wharf, shops, etc. I have a little house right on the shore. Hear the surf day and night. Gorgeous scenery.

Marvelous progress the last twenty-five years, especially in education. Qualified native teachers now, more roads, better conditions all over. Took a trip back into the bush where I worked twenty-five years ago. Much changed, of course, but I was touched at how many remembered me. These were the school kids then, grown now with families. Natives are affectionate and sentimental. It was nice indeed.

I have been spending my time clearing the jungle off the top of a hill with the help of four locals. It was a mess of overgrowth. I cannot do much, but I put in a few hours a day. It is about ready. I have been waiting for a lay missionary from England to come help me put up a small two room house on the hill top. The Bishop suggested this spot and he honors my desire for solitary life, etc. and has been fine. The missionaries are all dedicated hard-working men and women but very much outgoing, practical, driving sort of people. They simply cannot figure what I am up to, but they let it go at that for the most part. It is a poet in the midst of workers. I feel for that, a certain loneliness and longing for company, someone to talk to who could relate a little! It will be better I guess when I am by myself. I eat with them daily, but otherwise am by myself and have made one room into a chapel and do my office Oxford style and say Mass there. For the rest I read a lot.

I have good peace and feel right about everything and

feel there is a real need for this sort of thing here one way or other. In one sense this may be the best way to introduce the monastic life: begin with one. Had a group come I figure they would have set up a good "plant," begun a "business" and in general proved they knew what they were doing. But, I think, it would have so gotten off on the wrong foot. This way, at least, it is clear the thing is solitary, poor, ineffective, pointless, and rather dreamy-eyed. Which may be a bit closer to the reality, or at least the ideal. On the other hand, I feel there is real interest and in a certain way some challenge: it must be something to have someone come out here and settle in the midst of this action who has absolutely no plans whatever for doing anything! People seem warm enough to the idea, at least pose no problem.

I adjust happily to the climate so that is good. It is of course very much summer, and now quite a lot of rain. For all the "progress" it is a quiet place and one rarely sees or hears a plane go over and the mission boat comes in once a week or less, now and then a government boat. No phones, no television. There is radio contact between mission stations and headquarters a couple times a day, but I have little to do with that. A Sister cooks here, bakes bread, and a Brother at Alexishaven makes butter and sends it up. There is electricity from a generator each night till 9:30 P.M. (noisy machine) and ice box and they have fresh meat also from headquarters where there is a herd. Buildings are corrugated iron roof, fiberboard siding, wooden frame: good enough. Lots of flowers and shrubs.

I will get a little kerosene stove and icebox, do my own cooking, gardening, etc. I do not know what I will do to "earn" a living, though I did pick up a table loom in Australia. We'll see. I hope I can get going soon on my little house. I think I could have done it myself, but with no tools, equipment, etc. it would have been awkward. Meanwhile, it is not so bad.

I am sorry to have been so long sending a word. Give my love to all at home. I hear from Oxford and all seems well. I miss the place much. You will be coming into Spring soon now and that is a glorious season. I was always glad to see it come at the monastery. The Psalms ring pretty good here and I do not find it hard to find "meaning" in them! Of course I have my flute too and a set of Jung and the Britannica and a few other things so I am in good company.

You would like the people here. They are real, in touch with their heart, whole. They are such a contrast to the head-centered Westerners! I believe I owe my understanding of the monastic life more to them than to anything else. The whole primitive style was one foot on earth, one foot in the world of the spirit — in everything. What Western man offers them is pretty one-footed on earth and that's it. Even in religion there is little opening for the mystic dimension, very little. I think they need this kind of life here badly, even if not exactly the Trappist Cistercian style transplanted whole. My love to you and every good wish. Say a prayer that all goes well and that I do not drop the precious burden that I carry. There are seven missionaries of the old days buried up on the hill to keep me company. From 1904. Three of them lasted one year out here. Black water fever no doubt.

Peace in the Lord,
M. Kelty

5

May 24, 1974

Dear Bill:

How nice to hear from you. Your letter came today and I reply at once since I am in the mood. Yes, I think you made a good step; it is a pity we have sometimes to fight to keep our own freedom and our need for time and space, but it is something we must do if we would not be robbed of our birthright. Don't budge on solitude. It is essential. Some peace, some quiet, with everything turned off, the best stews are those that simmer a long time on the back of the stove. Hard to come by these days. No one cooks that way anymore. We are not that much better for it. I have grown deeper and deeper in my convictions on monastic life here and perhaps for the first time in my life have exposed to me the utter differences from the way of action. I certainly have not come to set all right and I have no reforming charism, but I guess being here is all I need to do.

There is a handsome and very excellent seminary program here but few indeed persevere. All are very heartbroken about it. Latest all the way, excellent staff, etc. But there is something wrong. I myself (I arrived yesterday!) suspect that it may be in the aggressive model of the priest that native fright arises. They are just not that kind of people. They are more whole, like Negroes at home who seem warmer, richer, more poetic, more romantic, more full of love for life and so lacking in that passion for production and profit that makes the successful man of the West. I think that's one reason they were so despised.

Anyway, I see a real need for this sort of thing (the

solitary life) here. But I am having to wait a long time to get settled. Only next week comes my young carpenter to start my little house. There may be some point in it. I never knew anything worth while that came off easily. I dip into I Ching now and then and get courage and get fine readings, encouraging me to hang on, dig in, bear up, go deeper. Meanwhile, here on the shore I have much time alone for prayer and reading and I have also met all the local Fathers and that is good. Gives me good insight into the scene. My, they are good men and work hard. In terms of Jung it is woman that is missing. They reject her: the compassion, tenderness, pity, feeling, awareness, grasp of beauty and loveliness — that is all missing. You cannot live without woman, that is for sure. The usual way is the real one; the monk's way, and the celibate's, is the inner one, no less real but on another dimension. But this gets small heed, I mean the cult of this inner side; and without it there is really no love life, which is to say prayer life, possible. I think the whole celibacy thing is rooted in the matter of solitude, but this has been given no heed. After all, only in recent years (through Merton) this was discovered; and in most seminaries even less, much less. Yet the celibate must live alone. If he has no understanding of it, how to use it, how to work through it to some sort of integrated life — what's he gonna do?

For all that, everyone, no matter what his state, needs some time alone, some hours of peace, of quiet; time to ponder and dwell with things, to let things be. For once we put our tools down and close our mouths and turn the lights out and the music off, and listen: to the wind, if you will. To the birds. To your own breathing. To the God hidden in the quiet of your own abandoned heart. Yes, sometimes it is hard, for, like the Psalms, all that comes out of the heart is not pretty. What did Christ say about what comes out of a man's heart? Yet we must come to know that if we are going to know what we are. And then to move on to call on God for His mercy and grace to heal us and help us. For we cannot tidy up our own hearts and make them sweet and pure: we are not capable of it. Instead, we ask Him in. For a long time I prayed at every Communion, "Come into the shambles of my heart, dear Lord; come into the shanty I call home." Well, he comes and turns everything he looks on to gold. But you can spend a lifetime prettying up the place and never manage; and since you never manage you never ask Him in. Pity. He wants in. But not even to know the human heart, this is a far worse tragedy, for it means you live in unreality, a fiction, out of touch with the truth. Then faith is reduced to formulas and prayer is just saying things and showing up when one should for one's own and others' edification. Yes, we need solitude in some form or other.

I am at peace. I am free. It is a beautiful country. I am alone, of no account, little, small potato, useless. No matter. I taste a good brew and am on to a good thing. Write again.

Love to all,
Matthew

6.

The following excerpts are taken from a letter Matthew had duplicated and sent to his friends. It also appeared in the Winter, 1974, issue of *Monastic Exchange*. Information and ideas appearing in other letters have been deleted.

August, 1974

Dear Friends:

This is a somewhat desperate attempt to catch up with time: desperate in that I am reduced to using this form of contact for the impossibility of handling it any other way. Even so, it means a generous service on the part of the monks of the Abbey of Gethsemani who typed, duplicated, and mailed this for me. My great thanks to them, and my long-delayed greetings to you by their courtesy.

I sit right on top of a hill several hundred feet high looking out over the Bogia plantation and the whole coastline of rolling hills and beaches of white edging the green fields and forests at their feet. There are four islands off Bogia, and another to the north twelve miles or so, 6,000 feet Manam, a volcano which has been very active this season. Most nights this past month or so there has been a huge torch of flame spouting out of the top and clouds of fine dust blowing north with the wind.

If you want to get to Madang, some hundred miles or so, you can take a ship if you like, if time is no problem and you do not mind sleeping on the deck; otherwise you can take the commercial plane that calls twice a week, or arrange for the mission plane to pick you up. All this amounts to remarkable service and an isolation that is really wild. All the same, it is a quiet spot, remote enough, and here on the hill, removed enough from the active scene to be a real haven for prayer and pondering. Which is just about all there is.

Not that there are things lacking to do! Just the chores from day to day take a lot of time. I keep my diet simple by choice and by circumstances, but it still leaves the food to be prepared. I keep the house neat and trim and if one man has few clothes to wash, the washing is a complex process when you haul the water and scrub on a board by hand. Some day I will have a garden, and there is probably more than I will be able to manage in keeping the grass down somehow and the brush prevented from growing up all around me. So far I have nothing more than a few dozen pineapple plants and the bananas growing in abundance here on the hill top. My staples are rice, cheese, fish, and a sort of soda-cracker (sea biscuits I call them); later on I may get a few chickens for eggs, and I can get abundant native vegetables and fruits, good and good for you, at the market down by the government station.

The house is two rooms; a main living room twelve by twelve, a chapel eight by twelve. In between there is a passage with a small section to each side about six by six for cooking (a two-burner kerosene stove) and for storing things. I have lots of windows, but in the end decided not to put in the louver windows we ordered; they block the glorious view and I thought I would try to get by with just the screens. First night, though, there was a great breeze blowing and went right through the house like a tunnel. I was cold and the next day had to go down and get another blanket from the store. Meanwhile I have rigged up some hanging partitions and blocked the passage-way and think I may be able to get by with that; it stops the wind and I still have the grand unimpeded view by day, since the breeze comes up high at night after sundown and lasts a few hours. During the day in sun a breeze feels good. The house sits on posts about two feet high, but hugs the ground since the roof is large, extending four feet over the sides of the house for shade. There is a porch six by twelve at the sea-side and a short, narrow one along the side for part of the way. It is a simple timber frame left exposed, with fiberboard sheeting for walls, and the roof is corrugated iron painted aluminum. We scraped the timber down smooth and varnished it and painted the sheeting white inside, so the inside looks very neat. And the ceiling has the timber beneath the sheeting, in oblong patterns; good-looking. Above the ceiling is some insulation that keeps the house cool even in days of brightest sunshine, though the iron roofing gets very hot.

One of the most dramatic aspects of being in a country like this is to be able for once to see what we of the West really amount to. Here somehow or other the whole thing seems to be up on display and it dawns on you in a new way how hideous is much of what we have done and much of what we really are. I am particularly disenchanted with the aggressive, pushy, self-assertive, grasping side of our scene. This is the way we are and this is the way we appear to the world. True, this very quality has made possible the outstanding achievements of the West, but it begins to dawn on us, and it is obvious to the young, that the same quality has done something dreadful to the spirit and has killed much in man that is essential to his happiness. We are surely not a tender, gentle, peaceful people. Nor are we kind and tolerant and loving. Nor reverent toward God or life or nature or the spirit within.

Now here in New Guinea I find the people themselves are of a mind with the monks. And so I have come here. I am the only monk in New Guinea. But I have come to say to these people: I am with you. For these are a spiritual people. True, the life of the spirit was not very developed. It was shot through with pragmatic aspects; a lot of it was one hand washing the other. Notwithstanding, their life was also permeated with religion; everything they did had a spiritual overtone, a relation to the other world. Whether they built a house, or dug a garden, or went hunting a pig, or held a sing-song, or went to war, it always involved contact with the other world, a relation to the spirits. They did not and do not live in this world only. In other words, they know they have a soul and they live as if the soul mattered.

Compared to them, the average Westener looks like a freak, a half-man, for no matter what he does, only one thing is sure; it will have no relation to the other world. He lives without reference to the soul. He pays no attention to his dreams. He does not listen to his heart. He does not sit under a tree and do nothing but look into space, infinite space.

It was New Guinea and the primitive life here that opened me up to the contemplative life. It was Thomas Merton who spelled it out for me. And Carl Jung who gave it all depth. And I have come back here to say thank you. And serve, in some way, if God so provides, for beginning the contemplative life of the Church here, even if doing so I do it alone. For doing it alone, be it noted, was the original way, the primitive monastic (monos: alone) experience; one could do worse.

For I see the contemplative life here as a natural. True, I do not see that you could import a Cistercian house here and expect things to develop; you would have to adapt and adjust and make it local. Perhaps the only ones who could do that would be the people themselves. Who knows? But at least a seed can be sown. An idea given. A suggestion made and a hint offered. Otherwise, if that aspect of the life of the Church is not present, we run not only the risk of having a Church which would be unbalanced and off-center, but also the ruin of a people. If these people lose their mystic quality we will have made them into our own image and likeness, we of the West, and I am not so sure that the image and likeness deserve repetition. Our own questions make that clear. No one is as disturbed at the way of the West as much as the Westerner. Listen to the young, or your own heart. Or your dreams.

So I feel I am where I belong and I hope I can swing it. I do not know how I am going to earn my keep. The Bishop says he will consider me part of the mission, but a monk likes to be on his own and make his own way. I'll try. Meanwhile I may need a little help. My day is the same as we used to have at the monastery at Oxford; I rise at three and begin my psalms and close with the Old Testament, have coffee and psalms and some Gospel at six and follow with Mass. Then another cup of coffee. In the morning I try to do some work around the place; there is enough to do. I eat something at noon, maybe take a little nap. In the afternoon I may do a little work or else read or write or pray. I get something to eat in the late afternoon and do the Vesper psalms about six, near sundown. After that I read for a couple of hours by the Coleman lamp; it is noisy but it is brighter and not so hard on the eyes. Bed around nine. It is a beautiful day. I practically live outdoors, close to the sea, the stars, the woods, the wind. Sometimes someone comes by and chats a bit; I show him the house. Maybe one of the Fathers or Brothers will drop by. Maybe not. Does not matter. I go visit the cemetery. Answer some mail. It is quiet, peaceful. I can think about things. About God. About me. Life. Time. Sin. Evil. The Church. Man. I feel very close to these people. I don't think I am fooling them. I suspect they know very well what I am about. Better than a lot of others.

Has not God been good to me? And is this not something wonderful to be doing? And is not this a wonderful place to do it? And is it not important? I rather think it is. Yes, social action is necessary. And the Church is much involved here, head over heels. Yet, something is to be said for the other side too. After all, if these people are to have everything that we have in the West, all the way down the line, they would have been better off before we came. For things are only things. Man is by nature a contemplative. When he is not he is sick. And a plethora of things is not going to help that sickness at all. Some of the unhappiest people I have known had everything. And these people are a lot healthier than the men of the West; they were even before we appeared. I'm for keeping them healthy.

My love to you, my good wishes, my blessings and prayers. Do you also think of me and pray that God be with me.

In Christ
Father Matthew Kelty
Monk of Gethsemani

7.

June 8, 1975

Dear Bill:
Thanks so much for the letter and the magazine which have just come. The article was very nice — too nice I should say — and it was really fun to read, bringing back all the happy memories of Oxford. My relationship to the place is a joy. I mean to say I have no regrets, no

heartache at not being there. It is rather a source of comfort and joy to me. It is good to know that it is there, that it continues, that I was and am — as it were — part of it. I wish there were Oxfords everywhere; maybe some day there will be. I am glad you have been up to see the monks, glad all is well. They sent me a painting of the dog and of a peacock; have them on my wall. Good indeed. I do believe I miss the dog most of all! Well, all right, the motorcycle, though I do have this little one here.

This is indeed a different sort of thing, though in some ways there is a touch of Oxford. I do have visitors and they do stay over sometimes and we do have excellent talk and we share the life. Some of the younger men have been a real grace to me. I declare the scene IS changing. I have my best talks with them; the "professionals" are so Western. I guess it is the aspect of solitude that makes it of a different sort. I take to it OK and seem to be able to manage all right. I do not say it is hard nor is it easy. How then? Maybe just say I feel it is real and that it is necessary to respond with all one has. Thus, there is some sort of satisfaction in the situation: I do nothing at all, really, and yet it all seems to make sense to me in some way or other. I do think you extend the experience of God and the self a bit further along the way. I do not mean any special "lights" and so on, just an overall awareness that is hard to define and slips through your fingers when you try to grasp it. Also, an entering into the human setting a bit more intensely. This is not much fun, but it does seem sound. It boils down to night and day. I guess it is a good idea to pray at night all right. You sort of move from one to the other: now pretty "down", now somewhat "up." I guess that's it: the tension of man's poverty/sinfulness and the beauty and

glory of God's love. One would like to go all one way —
this way or the other. It is keeping both in hand that
seems to be called for, the two poles I guess that weld
man to God, maybe two beams of the cross.

I really feel quite happy here, at peace. I still love
Gethsemani much and would not mind going back. Yet I
am content and at peace. It is just a matter of day by day
and oddly they seem very interesting to me, though at
day's end I daresay if I had to put on paper what I'd done
it would not amount to much. Nights are superb; dawns,
mornings elegant; sundown, evenings rich. You know
what the worst part of the day is? Around noon. Don't
know what it is: everything seems flat, killed and drench-
ed in white heat and light. Every bit of spirit seems to
vanish in that time. In one of the psalms there is a reference to the "noon-day demon." I think it is Psalm 90 of
the Vulgate. The old Latin had daemonio meridiano. I
know quite well what he speaks of; we used to sing that
psalm nights for Compline.

I do believe that all my theorizing on monastic obedience is sound. I quite agree that solitude can be
dangerous and hazardous: that one could bring one's self
with ease to doing things that are really off the track. I
have found great strength in my monastic bond and believe I would founder without it. True, I am not as it
were subject to an abbot on a day to day basis, but that
does not seem important. For all that, most monks are
not either. I mean day to day life takes care of itself, but
in the main drift, the general trend, quite another matter.

It boils down to a faith in God, I guess, as basic.
Which is really the point of monastic obedience. You
simply see the abbot as expressing the will of God. Or, as
the voice of the Church, which is again the will of God at
work. In other words, these are merely the foci on which

faith is oriented. Once this is clear and firm, then it is OK to open one's self to the experience of the human situation in depth, as they say. Which is what is happening everywhere anyway.

I just finished a book by a young girl who worked among the addicts and others at the very bottom of the London scene. Tragic. Old ones at the end of the line. Young ones just setting out. No question; there is a capacity for self-destruction, for self-hatred in man that is strong. A climate such as we live in brings it out, one of chaos and disintegration. And an era of little or perhaps no faith at all — really bad. What is to oppose the onslaught of self-contempt? Many of these young people literally destroy themselves, willingly, knowingly, even gladly, feeling a certain conviction in what they do as logical. Perhaps the cousin to this is violence, the same thing only transferred to others. I believe in solitude you get some taste of this formidable enemy, really the work of the evil one who leads us to the edge of despair and tempts us to jump. Only a strong gift of faith could answer that. I mean to say in God's love.

I had a youngster here not long back of almost no faith, deep into this very despair; break your heart to hear it come out of him. He had just one tiny glimmer of hope, for the only reason he kept going was there might be something "beyond." We have no idea of what a power and grace and joy faith is. Nor the horrors to which those without faith are exposed.

I guess faith is from the mother; by her unquestioning love we learn to believe in love. From that faith comes action, and that makes us like the father. Action follows from faith, does not precede it. There is something feminine in faith. Something masculine in action. I think we need the stress of the feminine; it has been neglected. The

Church needs to be more Mother; the role of the Virgin Mary will necessarily grow. The union of Christ with Church, of identity with her, union with her is to be like Him in total faith, like Him in the action that follows from faith. In the end, I guess faith is the action. "This is the work of God, to believe," He said. The work we are to do. We are too much action, too little believing. We like independence; not dependence. We substitute action for believing, but I don't think we can get away with it. There is no ring in it. Hollow.

I sense a certain amount of that in reaction to my being here; I mean I really don't DO anything. Oddly enough this for some reason raises questions. What does all the action amount to? Perhaps the answer is: not much. Obviously, pointing this out, as it were, is not always highly appreciated! I am aware of this. I still maintain that the finest thing a man can do is to face up to the total truth of his own reality and of the reality all around him and in response make an act of faith in God's love.

Which is the why of real prayer, for it opens us to the total aspect of the human state, makes us aware of what we really are, thus necessarily deepens faith. It is this faith deepened by an experience of poverty and need that rouses in man those qualities of tenderness and compassion that make him a real Christian, not just a "stout believer." We have priests by the score whose theological faith is proper and perfect, but all in the head, and really quite heartless. There is no humanity to it, no experience of human misery. And thus the miserable find no compassionate chord to relate to. Faith then seems to be impossible, something they can never do. Ideally, the monk's experience of prayer would lead him to such a desert scene as to wake him up to what being a human is really like, thus calling forth deeper faith. The fruit would be a man of compassion and tenderness.

But my point is that the world itself is a desert today. No one has to become a monk to enter it. But like the monk we ought as Christians to respond to the scene not with a program, but with a faith that can stand in the midst of chaos and firmly believe that back of it all is a loving God. And that the surrounding chaos is nothing new. We have been carrying it around within us all the while. Because we deliberately and coyly ignored it, God exposed it for all to see. Hence, as He said, "Will there be faith in the last days?" Well, Lord, if these are those the answer is, not much. To which He would reply, And you?

Which is why I think there is no better gift today. Nor do I believe it hard to come by. In fact, it is had for nothing. One need only beg for it.

There are women who love their man that way, I mean a woman who will stick with a man long after everyone else has given him up for dead loss. There is something touching in such loyalty, such love, such faith. I think we have to be like that. When God does all He cares to do, we have still to be able to smile and say, "I love you anyway and always will. I believe in you and always shall." So, when we face the desert scene, within and without, we respond with faith, rejecting the demon of darkness and despair.

There is a teacher in the village where I was 25 years ago; a catechist for many years. A good, faithful soul. Raised a fine family. He is sort of retired now. Lives on the station as kind of senior, honored citizen. Kids have grown up; one as a nurse, one a teacher, one a nun. Real fine couple. When you realize his father and mother were bush people, etc., you see a great movement. Faithful, zealous, a real man of prayer, for I accidentally discovered him many times at odd hours at night in chapel. So now he is a revered old man, much loved. He gets a bit sick, they send him down to Madang to hospital to check. He comes back now. Now what? He has leprosy.

Honestly, is this the way He treats His friends?

Do you see what I mean?

The man? He smiles, is at peace. God is good. Has eight children, pleased for that.

My, this is too long, too long. Love to you and all the family. Hope all is well. Every good wish. Keep in touch.

Matthew Kelty

8.

The following excerpts are from another duplicated newsletter, mailed from New Guinea by Matthew.

January, 1976

Greetings!

So what is new? Not much, really. I am (1) still here, (2) still alive and well, (3) as content as when I came, now two years ago. I have been installed here in my house on the hill a year and a half and have grown rather accustomed to the place, worked into it. There has not been much external change to report. I did close in the porch and make a chapel of it, using the former chapel space as living area; it is better so. I have a large cross erected on the hill outside the house, maybe 25 feet high. We put it up on Holy Cross day, which was close to Independence Day here, so it is properly identified. I have a treadle

Singer sewing machine, which I use now and then. And a large loom which I do not have in working order yet. I do not know as much else is different, save the dog, rather much a Labrador and very much a friend and companion. Devoted. She enjoys riding the motorcycle, sitting on the seat before me, paws on the handlebars.

Christmas I went back to one of the bush stations to do the Christmas Masses. A Father back there is holding down two places and it seemed a reasonable exception to my usual apartness from ministry. It was pleasant enough, even if the 14 miles of road in and out was much a mess. One thinks of these youths who make a great sport of tracking hill and hollow, through streams, up banks, plunging into mud and bogging — find it a lark and an achievement, expertise on a bike. I am happy to be able to manage and admire the men and women who take it here as a matter of course. There are three Fathers using this road, and on and off there are lay missionaries, nurses, teachers, and so on who are part of the staff. Some half of the year it is navigable by jeep. It serves a wide area of scattered villages. These people walk, unless they can get a ride on a government or mission jeep. Only a few teachers can afford motorbikes.

Many of the missionaries here do not realize what a wonderful work they do. They are much aware of their own failings, and suffer acutely from them. They are neither overly impressed with themselves or the work done. In fact, they are perhaps too harsh. They forget that the Church has always been human, that human frailty and stupidity have always been there. But within that human poverty something divine is at work, hidden, secret. The Church has been planted here, it has taken root, it grows. That is the main thing. The chief work has been done. That does not not mean there is no work to be done now, but one can pause long enough to rejoice in the taking root. Everything enters a new stage now.

One gets the impression ever more strongly that the most significant action out here is (in terms of import) the Church. It is closely in touch with the people; more than that it reaches deep into areas that really matter. It is without doubt the agent of greatest point, for it is concerned with immortality, eternal life. No one belittles progress in the temporal, least of all in the name of religion, but it is purblind to follow a general assumption that the good life on earth is the road to happiness. One could imagine immersing the local cultures in Christ, leaving the core basically intact while enriching and developing it. Our own forebears long ago were introduced to the Faith with a minimum of imported change: "development" followed after, and slowly. But in the dazzle of much that is externally impressive here, it is difficult to keep one's vision, when everyone else is a hustler with commerce, education, industry, health, transport, agriculture . . . it is awkward to be found pushing prayer and mysticism. However, no one is fooling me. The West has everything it wants and yet starves to death for life in the spirit. Man is a great deal more than money and what money can buy. However, we all of us have a trend to idolatry and the love of false gods. It can do us no harm to reckon with that. For all that, the people of Papua New Guinea, too, tend to worship Mammon; we are all kin, sons of Adam. Yet, the Church is here, it proclaims something. A community of contemplative monks would be a great good in this land, also proclaiming something and perhaps more likely to be heard for their being silent. And practically useless.

Beyond the amazing beauty of this country, it is the people who are most fascinating. The loveliness of the land is obvious; it takes a bit longer to see the depth of a people who have been here thirty thousand years or longer and who developed a way of life that functioned. Europeans tend to forget that we ourselves were primitives only a short time ago. Our "history" is relatively short. That these people have gone through such staggering changes in so remarkably brief a time and have not broken manifests a profound strength. When one thinks of the great fuss we make over changes (even minor ones in the Church) in the last generation or so, one's admiration for these people only mounts. They make do somehow. Further, one can learn from them, learn a great deal. It is commonly assumed, also by the government, that foreigners come here to do some service for the people. I must say that in my own case I have as much in mind my own good as anything else. To be sure, I do not come to make money or to profit in some material way, but what one can gain in insight into human nature, the human dimension, is priceless. Here it is clear that man is a spiritual being, has a contemplative nature, lives in two worlds, not one. These people are kin to wind and weather, the night, silence, the voices that surround one from bush and tree and brook and sea. It is not necessary to glamorize them or to blind to much that is unworthy. On the other hand, it is necessary to move beyond what seems to be impoverished or even degraded primitive ways, for they are deeper than they look. Their culture is intricate and sophisticated. Even for one ignorant of the skills needed to unravel and explicate local ways, it is good just to watch them, talk to them, listen to them. I really do not see that much of them, it is true, least of all in any traditional setting, but in another way I am favored in that I have no official role which might tend to reduce everything to patterns in communication. I do not fit into any category.

I will go down to Alexishaven soon and take care of mimeographing this and send it out. My teeth need attention and the dentist Brother is there at this time of year. I will also get a few things I need, possibly a power mower so I can do something about the sleezy look this hilltop has. Though people seem to be moving about at will, travel this season is usually unreliable. Rains so far, though, have not been excessive.

I think of you often. In the time and quiet and solitude I have one dwells on many things. I look out over the sea, the world, and also the world I have known. Life gets shorter as you live longer. It is brief at best. One laughs and shakes one's head over much, but the mercy of God absorbs our absurdity. Only then can one afford to laugh at one's self. Peace and joy!

Matthew Kelty

9.

January 29, 1977

Dear Bill and family:

Thanks for your letter just come; nice to receive word from you and glad too all is well with you. I am sorry to return your love by no more than such an air letter, but I had better get something down. Mail is something of a problem, but I must say so with candor that I enjoy getting letters. It follows I should answer with same spirit, right?

Christmas time the mail was heavy and also surface mail came through, so I got a batch of papers and books that have long been on the way. One of the books I just got was *The Sexual Celibate* by Donald Goergen, a young Dominican, very sharp. I hope it comes out in paperback. It is very refreshing and says a lot of things I have stumbled on one way or the other, but says them professionally and with much learned background. It gave me much joy. I hope it gets a good reception. Also got *Poustinia* by Catherine Doherty. This is on the spiritual life, especially the use of solitude as based on Russian tradition. She has a Russian background and founded a lay movement in Canada after some experience in the USA. Fine woman. Merton knew her. You have probably seen Raymond Bailey's *Thomas Merton on Mysticism*. I have not read it yet, but it looks fine: a Baptist minister. Then I got *The Pilgrim at Tinker Creek*, which for the bit I have read is a joyous thing. I got Zaehner's *Our Savage God* which is a bit wild but says a lot of things I like. Maybe you can get these books in your college library. Books run so high. So I have some good things to read. Now I recall telling you all this on a newsletter I just did, but it will go sea mail and so be six months maybe reaching you!

I am back from a visit to the Highlands and weaving center there with the lepers. Fine trip, several hundred miles over unbelievable roads. After all, the mountains rise up to 14,000 feet. Many more people up there, more than here: vigorous, enterprising. Mission is well built up and rather advanced. Some of the places look like parishes in the USA. Do nice weaving, using some local wool, too, including spinning, dyeing. Learned a lot. I was last up there in 1951, so it was dramatic to note changes. Then back to get my teeth fixed and up the coast 14 hours on the boat. All is well here and I was glad to get back.

I am content and at peace. Yes, I think solitude tends to open one to basic things. I think moving from active ministry, to contemplative monastery to Oxford to here has been a slow thing, but all of a piece. Among other areas a reconciling or absorbing of the other side of man and all the consequences. That's why this book above hit me so hard; it confirmed me in what I have come to know myself. And of course this sort of life does expose one to human poverty and the need of mercy, opens one to the mystery of the human heart, the universal heart. It has at times been a rather difficult thing, but it always comes into shape and right now I have only gratitude for it all. I do sometimes feel that I may be moving into something else, but I have no notion what nor do I fuss around with anything like dreams or plans or projects. I live from day to day and let it go at that.

I think the role of obedience is to help us to remain loyal to the truth and to help us discover God's truth, another way of saying, our own. That problem, in our terms, is always the false self, the make-believe self, the self we have constructed. This is a relatively harmless business in a life of no great depth or intensity, but once you move into something a little serious, it can become a snag. The role of the monastic obedience was to shake one free of the dominance of the "ego," the false self, the worldly self. When well handled on both sides, it works, of course. The role of the Church can be seen in a somewhat similar light in that it limits, defines, orients the work of the Spirit and keeps us from worshipping a spirit which we gladly assume to be divine because it is ours. Certainly in your own life obedience is just as vital in that you must, if you are to attain to your freedom, your destiny, respond wholly to God's will, which is to say, be truly yourself. The problem lies in trying to discern that true self, to find freedom road and walk it. Here we are much deceived often enough, assuming that we know who we are and what we are to do. Thus, there is to be some sort of deference to God's will that is almost total: I say almost total to indicate that it is not mere "submission" but something we "work out," we do, we unravel day by day. Purity of heart, as the old monks used to say, is the secret. Being clean. Not devious or scheming. Honest in everything. I am quite sure that God's will can be discerned, and correctly, but one must be totally open to whatever it be, available. (This is a rather feminine quality for a man.) God makes His will known, that is sure. And we follow it with conviction.

So we pray in that direction: Thy will be done. In the end my will and His are one, which is to say, my deepest self is God's will. I myself and His will for me are identified. That is why doing His will can never be thought of save as the road to freedom, to fulfillment, to perfect response to our destiny, our being. There is no greater joy. But the pursuit of this can be pretty rough. Among other things there is the absolute need for a grasp of what we truly are, in the widest sense (the whole self), the good and the bad, an acceptance of that and an entry with that into God's mercy. Or the other way around, to experience God's mercy overwhelming us. The greater the knowledge of human misery (our own, the communal) the greater the intensity of the experience of God's merciful love. From then on there is nothing but the desire to enter into His holy will wholly, entirely. It is the response to love received.

I think you know very well what I speak of and know what it means to be called to something, to know one must do it, to do it, and to rejoice in having done it, even if the doing meant considerable suffering, misunderstanding, etc., etc. Darkness is part of it, hope, risk, but I believe in the end it all works out if you keep it clean, free, unselfish, open. I think a man needs superb relation to woman to do this, the woman within, embraced at last through the love of his spouse who gently leads him to be himself, a person, a being of great love.

Well, let it be. God is very good. Love to all.

Matthew Kelty

10.

The opening paragraph of this letter refers to a group of college students that has traveled from eastern North Carolina to Gethsemani for annual retreats.

June 28, 1976

Dear Bill:

Thanks a lot for your letter; I enjoyed it very much. Anyone (or any group) that will drive fourteen and a half hours to Gethsemani — well. It may say something for Gethsemani, but it says a great deal about one aspect of the American scene today, does it not?

The abbot wants me to go to the Philippines monastery for a month or two to get a taste of life in community again. Sounds OK though it seems I just got here. I am two years on the hill; it is three years since I officially left Gethsemani, though I did not leave Oxford till October, 1973. Been in Papua New Guinea two and a half years; it goes fast. However, one plays it free. I have discovered it is better not to be attached to anything.

The life continues to be good. That is rewarding, if

that is the word. It seems to be mostly Simone Weil's *Waiting for God*. I do little then. You just never know what the day will bring, or the night. I guess the point of this apartness is that there is not much of anything to serve as diversion and you simply become more aware of what is part of normal life anyway, but gets crowded out. It is like the weather; it is now good, now bad. Sometimes glad it is over, sometimes glad it isn't. And you neither fight it or pursue it. You let it be, let it come. I guess that is why the receptive side is important, as I noted: the taming of dominance, the cult of acceptance. I mean too much effort, discipline, regimen, routine, performance, duty, etc., etc. All very good and satisfying, but it can create an unbalance. What seems optimum is when the stage is reached that everything flows smooth and easy, you are used to things, can move dexterously through the day without much effort. Then the acceptance can enter in and be strong.

That is the trouble with the past few years: too much fuss and fury over externals, constant change, improvement, tinkering, burns up all your energy keeping up with it. Even trying too hard with liturgy, always coming up with something better. Gethsemani was and I suppose still is breathtaking in many ways; a fascinating place I found it. But there is some point in things being dull too. Even boring. I find I return to my childhood and a capacity for sitting and looking. I do not think it is a reversion; perhaps a recovery. Or rebirth. However, it is not a constant and I am accustomed to agitation. And am stimulated at once in this direction by people.

Odd scene. Seems to me that I am so different alone and with others that I feel guilty about it after converse. Or shun converse and then people are hurt. But then I find I need it anyway and so I conclude that it is just two

119

dimensions to one whole. So I conclude that love must always leave room for silence as for speech, for together and apart. God has many voices, many faces. Indeed, many moods. There was a song once, "Two Loves Have I . . ." and the theme was: both of them are you. Something to it. I guess we need to know our other side if we are to be whole. The side that Greeley says Western man knows nothing of. I see no need to be weird. I would rather be normal, whole. There is time for everything, a time for doing and a time for doing nothing. A time to hurry up and a time to wait. Well, now time to stop and send love to you and all of yours. Peace and joy.

Matthew

11.

In the summer of 1976 I wrote to Matthew and asked if he would object to my doing a little book about his journey to solitude. Although I had some of his personal papers, there were a number of questions I had to ask. The following letter was his response.

August 4, 1976

Dear Bill:

Thanks for your letter just come; also for the gift enclosed. A kindly act for which I am greatful, though you know your love needs no support.

I had forgotten that I had dabbled with the notion of going off anyway, no matter what. There were some who counselled so, the idea being that if you were called, you were called, and nothing should stand in the way.

Almost identified it with courage, while not acting it out was timidity. And some have done it so. Monks leave for other avenues and sometimes do so without reference to the abbot's wishes. They just make up their minds and ask release. But I could never bring myself to this. It went against the whole grain of my approach to monastic life, and anyway, I did not trust myself that much. I am a bit romantic and imaginative: such people get carried away with their own visions. I think submission to the abba in the spirit is elemental. Most of all when it gets to something as serious or as basic as such a change, for it was a change within the context of the monastic life, but continuing in it, even deeper, one hopes, and so it seemed to me in the end impossible to think one could do such independently of the abbot. Anyway, that is the way I worked it out and I stuck to that.

Why not just write as you feel and not be too concerned with whether it is private or not, etc. Most of this seems all right with me. None of this is painful to me or anything like that. I think all worked out in the providence of God. The abbot did OK by me. The Oxford experience was superb and perfect toward coming here. In fact, coming here has been just a pulling together of everything and a good peace. I suppose it comes to accepting yourself wholly in God.

All of this would strike anyone in his right mind as being dreadfully lacking in modesty. Fancy someone taking seriously a paper on himself! Still, I shrug, indifferent. It may help someone. It means nothing to me one way or the other. The whole question amuses me. In the SVD we were always working for publicity, had a public relations man and tried hard to publicize our work. When I was at Oxford we did nothing, could not have cared less. But all the papers were out and did big pages on the place, unasked. Nor did it do us harm. They always did a good job, I thought.

I am glad your group continues. I really do believe we are on the edge of a great period. I think it will be painful and arduous, but of great ultimate benefit. I feel the West will turn inward and amalgamate inner and outer in a way never done before, the meeting, wedding, of East and West.

I believe the Reformation was a start in this direction, but it did not come off. We were not ready for it. Now perhaps we are. Meanwhile, the outer has advanced beyond wildest imaginings and thus the inner turn will be all the more marvelous and deep, though of course for the same reason very difficult. This is why I make much of authority, not in the sense of an ism, but of the testing of the Spirit, lest we be betrayed. The inner journey needs good guidance.

Love to you and every good wish. Best regards to all.

Matthew

12.

January 31, 1977

Dear Bill:

Thanks for your letter; it was waiting for me when I got back from the Philippines just a bit ago. It is good to be back. Very good. I enjoyed my visit and found the Philippines monastery a charming place, but I feel I belong here. The place is like Oxford in many ways. It is all in Filipino style, thatch roofs, bamboo walls and siding, etc. And since there are about twenty monks there and only four are USA monks, it looks very much a part of the place. And the food is Filipino. Rice and smelly fish! They raise pigs for sale and are doing OK. Also grapes, nuts, and grow their own rice, vegetables, bananas, etc. Have about sixty goats and some similar number of ducks for eggs. They thought of milk from the goats, but the grass is not good enough. They do keep the hill clean and that avoids fire — a hazard. They pump water by windmill and also gather the pig manure for methane to cook by. Clever, these monks.

It was good to get away for awhile; gives me a chance to rethink things and see them in perspective. So far I am only confirmed in what I am doing, or perhaps better in what I am not doing, and find great peace in this. Still, it is not without its odd quality. I mean I am really doing nothing. It seems a strange role. Maybe the only thing that holds it together is some notion that it is the monastic life in miniature. To come down to it, the monk too does "nothing," though I must say that when there are one hundred of them doing it, it is a bit more impressive! I feel no call whatever to implement something, to get something started. Maybe this is only fear or cowardice or simple laziness, but that is where I am at. On the other hand, just being here doing this has its own attraction and I truly feel some significance in it and a sort of reality that I find in no other context. At least for me, doing it alone is the best way. I am simply carried out of inner concern too much when I am with a lot of others. I do not know how healthy this is, how sound, but that is how I put it.

Not that I do not enjoy people. I do. But when I forego company I become something else, or am aware of something more. In fact, I feel I get closer to them and to basic truth that way. So I conclude that this is what I am supposed to do, or perhaps, all that I can do. Trouble is, I guess, that what goes on within is more real to me than what goes on without. And I can only relate to it in a context of solitude. I assume that characterizes a call to this sort of life. But I do not spend time explaining it to myself or others. I am tired of that. Anyway it seems without point. As is usually the case with me, I do something first and then try to find out why afterwards! You be what you be I guess, like it or lump it and in that find peace. Naturally, you try to make it sound very reasonable! Not too easy. A woman trying to explain why she bought the dress. If you can get it "blessed" that helps, of course, gives it some sort of status. In the context of faith that means it is seen as the confirmed will of God. And the blessing I have. So I should worry further?

For a while there I was afraid I was going to lose it and that when I got to the Philippines I would be confronted with a situation in which it became evident to me that I belonged there. I was prepared for that, at some cost. But when I got there, it was not so. I felt no such call. So I ended up getting back what I was willing to give away.

I guess that is why coming back here was such a happiness. Flying into Madang was a right pretty scene for me, and the place sure looked good. And this place even better. And everything is just fine. No one bothered anything. Pretty good deal, figuring this place sits isolated on a hill. And people do steal. So, all is well. I hope with you too. Regards to your family and my love to any about who know the name. And if you go to Oxford, my best.

Matthew

13

May 31, 1977

Dear Bill P.:

You are there and back by now — Greece, I mean — and I hope all went nicely, that there were no mishaps and that you enjoyed the exposure to what I take to be a very lovely land.

The reports begin to come of the abbots in chapter. They seem a stimulating group and I feel very much out of things when I read of their discussions and their concerns. And odd comments, like the remark of the abbot general of the Benedictines, speaking of the need for roots, that he was not long ago in an Austrian monastery with an uninterrupted history of 1200 years! Fancy living in a house with that background! One would think of "tradition" in massive terms, I would think. Then the house in the Philippines, five years old!

You get to understand something of the earlier monks of the desert in this scene. It is no desert to be sure, everything is wildly luxuriant and there is green growth everywhere, with stuff of unbounded vigor bursting out all over. There is this: the warmth. I note you can get by eating very little indeed. I was never any good at fasting, but here there is nothing to it. Colder climates demand energy and thus food. Here you do not need all that. And the climate slows you down. So you end up more relaxed — though relaxed is perhaps a bit too strong for me — yet more slow and easy-going. Most Europeans seem extraordinarily rushed in this climate; they are no more so than back home, but it shows up here. You begin to see how less food and less stimulating environment tends to peace. Yet the mind seems active enough and you can have good insights and so on. But I think it is also a lot more passive, more receptive. Not quite so aggressive.

I guess that is why as monastic life moved north into the woods of Europe it got to be a lot busier than anything the South had — meaning down toward warmer lands. Maybe that is why the Celtic monks were an intense crew, given to extremes of discipline and ascetic endeavor. And a restless bunch wandering all over Europe and wrangling no end over this and that, like when is Easter.

You see the locals sitting watching the Europeans go whizzing by. I think they are dazzled by all the motion. I remember once when I was down at the mission, I took the bike and went over to the government center to get something at the store. There was an old man sitting on the steps. I got what I wanted and then came back. But I no sooner had done so than I remembered I forgot to get something, so I promptly got on the bike and went back to get it. I went in and when I came out, the old man was sitting there chuckling to himself almost uncontrollably. He wasn't trying to be nasty, he just couldn't help it. I said, "What are you so happy about?" He told me, "You came roaring up here and got something and went roaring out. And then in a minute later you came roaring back!" The local, of course, would very slowly walk over, linger long in buying, hang around a while, and then very slowly wander back. Might take him an hour or two. The scene tickled me. We must present a weird show to them.

Soon as I am with Europeans, as we call them, I am back in style, but here by myself I go slow and it is easy to do so. Flows from the structure of things. Or else I am slowly getting lazier and lazier and calling it spiritual growth!

I should labor you with all this small talk. The Lord's peace be with you. And blessings on your labors.

Matthew